RichThoughts
for Breakfast
Volume 6

Harold Herring

President of The Debt Free Army
& RichThoughts TV

www.HaroldHerring.com

Debt Free Army
PO Box 900000, Fort Worth, TX 76161

RichThoughts for Breakfast Volume 6
by Harold Herring

ISBN: 978-0-9763668-7-4
Copyright © 2019 by the Debt Free Army
PO Box 900000, Fort Worth, TX 76161
817-222-0011
harold@haroldherring.com

Unless otherwise noted, Scripture references are taken from the King James Version of the Bible.

Please obtain consent of the Author prior to any reproduction, whether in whole or in part, in any form.

Printed in the United States of America.
All rights reserved.

RichThoughts for Breakfast
Volume 6
Table of Contents

Day	Title	Page
1	Stop Economic Terrorism	7
2	12 Great Things About John 3:16	15
3	7 Ways to Get Rid of the Scum	23
4	8 Things I Will Always Remember	31
5	If You're Doing It … Stop It	39
6	3 Things to Know in Battle	48
7	It's Your Character, Not Your Checkbook Balance	56
8	Don't Say That	64
9	Imagine or Living the Good Life	71
10	How Free Are You?	79
11	7, 8 or 9 Things You Will Like	87
12	He Feels What You Feel	94
13	Are You in a Tight Spot?	101
14	5 Things to Know Before You Invest	109
15	7 Keys to Your Immediate Financial Release	117
16	7 Ways to Show You Really Love the Lord	125
17	Success Secrets of Jesus	133
18	The Successful Leadership Secrets of Jesus	143
19	The Greatest Mathematician I Ever Met	151
20	God Is Not Weak (or Showdown at Mt. Carmel)	159
21	It's Not Behind You – It's in Front of You	166
22	Ask the Right Person the Right Questions	174
23	Finding Peace in a Troubled World	182
24	Promises to Keep Before I Sleep	190
25	You Don't Need to Know It all	198
26	Nobody Could Ever Love Somebody Like Me	206
27	7 Reasons to Do What Is Good	213
28	7 Reasons Fear Destroys the Anointing	220
29	7 Steps to a Righteous Life	228

Day 1

Stop Economic Terrorism

Welcome to *RichThoughts for Breakfast*, the first day of your year of unfilled promises BEING FULFILLED.

If you ever found yourself wondering whether or not you can make all your monthly payments or how much longer before you get the foreclosure or eviction notice ... then you know what it's like to live in financial terror.

Isaiah 33:18 in The Living Bible says:

> "Your mind will think back to this time of terror when the Assyrian officers outside your walls are counting your towers and estimating how much they will get from your fallen city."

Make no mistake about it, **the credit card companies**, the money lenders, and the interest junkies know exactly how much money they will make on you. They understand every aspect of your financial life.

If you're in debt ... your life is not your own. Not only

7

that, **but your money is going to make somebody else rich.** Consider these four facts.

The average consumer has a total of 13 credit obligations on record at a credit bureau.

The average credit card debt per household with credit card debt in 2013 was $15,162.

Two penalty fees from credit cards ... late fees and exceeding the credit limit ... add up to $12.5 billion.

That year ... actually reached $20 billion dollars before legislation restricted the over the limit fees.

However, the banks weren't interested in losing money so the fees charged to merchants doubled from $24 billion in 2008 to $48 billion in 2011. By the way, that averages out to $467 per household.

Make no mistake about it ... these additional charges are being passed on to us, the consumers.

I want to go back to the $12.5 billion paid for just two fees ... this does not even count the amount that was paid in interest.

I want you to catch this next point ... $12.5 billion paid in credit card fees is misplaced stewardship ... **and I can tell you** that God's not happy about how we're using His resources.

I can assure you that the money lenders and credit

purveyors **can tell you exactly how much they will profit from in fees and interest**. It becomes a matter of averages and it's highly profitable ... for the economic terrorists.

You might think I'm being too hard by calling the money lenders economic terrorists.

According to the Random House Dictionary the word terrorist means:

"a person who terrorizes or frightens others."

Many unsuspecting believers (yes, they should know better, but they don't) <u>are daily being seduced into debt by alluring ads promising the good life</u> ... *yet, none of these ads ever talk about the consequences of not being able to pay your bills*.

That's a frightening scenario for believers who are in debt.

I personally think credit cards should carry a warning label just like cigarettes. *Smoke will kill you* **but so will the stress of not being able to pay off your debts <u>and/or provide for your family</u>**.

For me, it's not a stretch to call indiscriminate money lenders or anyone who extends credit without any regard as to the person's ability to service their debt ... economic terrorists ... because they're wreaking havoc on families around the world.

Isaiah 33:19 in The Living Bible says:

> "But soon they will all be gone. These fierce, violent people with a strange, jabbering language you can't understand will disappear."

Financial deliverance is coming to the children of God. I've have been anointed, appointed and equipped to help deliver believers out of the bondage of debt and lack.

One of my favorite scriptures is Exodus 14:13 which in the Message Bible says:

> "Moses answered the people, 'Do not be afraid. Stand firm and you will see the deliverance the LORD will bring you today. The Egyptians you see today you will never see again.'"

Financial deliverance is coming to the home of every person reading this. Believe it. Confess it. Expect it. The manifestation is on the way ... and you will never see the Egyptians (economic terrorists) again.

Isaiah 33:20 in The Living Bible says:

> "Instead you will see Jerusalem at peace, a place where God is worshiped, a city quiet and unmoved."

It's time for you to put yourself in a position where you can hear the voice of God. If you're surrounded by money lenders ... all you're hearing is the noise about the advantages of this product or that.

When you're no longer worried about answering the phone or opening the door for fear of the repo man or a process server showing up … **then you will find a real peace** *where you can focus on His voice … instead of any other.*

Isaiah 33:20 in The Living Bible says:

> *"The glorious Lord will be to us as a wide river of protection, and no enemy can cross."*

You may have faced or may be facing a Financial 9-1-1 … as a result of economic terrorism *but you've got to know* that God is your personal place of refuge, comfort, strength, direction and power.

You ought to be shouting as you hear verse 20 knowing that God will not only protect you against every attack of the enemy … <u>but He will place a hedge of protection around you</u> … keeping you safe from all harm.

Hallelujah.

I recently heard Pastor Bill Winston make a profound political observation. He said that the United States Supreme Court is not the highest court in our nation or any other nation in the world for that matter.

Truthfully, I've read through the Bible dozens and dozens of times, but I never really saw the contemporary significance of Isaiah 33:22 in The Living Bible which says:

> "For the Lord is our Judge, our Lawgiver and our King; he will care for us and save us."

Now catch this parallel. **God is our Judge (judicial branch of the government); God is our lawgiver (legislative branch) and He is our King (executive branch.)**

There is no compromise in these three members of the Godhead ... <u>ethics are not situational</u> ... you don't do your own thing. Not at all ... if we want to survive and thrive on planet earth.

When we put our faith, hope, trust and confidence in the Lord ... He will give us victory in every situation we face ... and our enemies will flee.

Isaiah 33:23 in The Living Bible says:

> "The enemies' sails hang loose on broken masts with useless tackle. Their treasure will be divided by the people of God; even the lame will win their share."

Are you getting hold of the last part of this scripture? It says that <u>"their treasure will be divided by the people of God."</u>

Hallelujah!! The wealth of the wicked is laid up for the righteous. There are several scriptures that remove all doubt about where the wealth of the wicked is headed

… it's into my house.

Proverbs 13:22 says:

> *"A good man leaveth an inheritance to his children's children: and THE WEALTH OF THE SINNER IS LAID UP FOR THE JUST."*

Ecclesiastes 2:26 says:

> *"For God giveth to a man that is good in his sight wisdom, and knowledge, and joy: but to the sinner he giveth travail, TO GATHER AND TO HEAP UP, THAT HE MAY GIVE TO HIM THAT IS GOOD BEFORE GOD."*

Job 27:16-17 says:

> *"Though he heap up silver as dust, and prepare raiment as the clay; He may prepare it, but the just shall put it on, and THE INNOCENT SHALL DIVIDE THE SILVER."*

Think about this … remember the $12.5 billion dollars paid in fees to credit card companies … where do you think that money's REALLY going? Hallelujah. And that's just the beginning.

Isaiah 33:24 in the Contemporary English Version of the Bible gives you and every other believer even greater benefits than anything financial.

"The LORD will forgive your sins, and none of

you will say, 'I feel sick.'"

Talk about blessed assurance. The Lord *"will forgive your sins."* Period. Paragraph.

Now get ready for this ... *"none of you will say, I feel sick."* Not only will you not get sick ... **you will not even feel sick**.

Our journey through Isaiah 33 concludes with the knowledge, the commitment and assurance <u>that you've got money, forgiveness and healing coming your way</u>.

Thank you, Jesus.

Day 2

12 Great Things About John 3:16

The very first Bible verse I ever memorized was John 3:16. I'm sure that's probably <u>the same with nearly every child raised in a Christian home</u> or who had any exposure to the Word of God.

It is a *universal picture of a merciful God <u>who willingly sacrificed His Son</u> for our sins <u>because of His unmatched love for us</u>*.

Would it surprise you to know the words forming John 3:16 contain 12 of the greatest blessings you could ever imagine?

John 3:16 says:

> "For God so loved the world, that he gave his only begotten Son, that whosoever believeth in him should not perish, but have everlasting life."

For God ... *the greatest period ... paragraph.*

So loved ... *the greatest concern.*

The world ... *the greatest distance.*

That He gave ... *the greatest single act.*

His only begotten Son ... *the greatest gift.*

That whosoever ... *the greatest opportunity.*

Believeth ... *the greatest act of faith.*

In Him ... *the greatest attraction.*

Should not perish ... *the greatest promise.*

But ... *the greatest difference.*

Have ... *the greatest assurance.*

Everlasting life ... *the greatest future possession.*

<u>Let's look at each of these individually to give them the full attention they deserve.</u>

1.   For God ... the greatest

Genesis 1:1 in the New Living Translation says:

"In the beginning God created the heavens and the earth."

Revelation 22:13 says:

"I am the Alpha and the Omega, the First and

the Last, the Beginning and the End."

God is the beginning and the end ... all that is, was or ever will be ... the Alpha and the Omega. He is God and there is none like Him.

2. So loved ... the greatest concern

I Timothy 2:4 says:

> *"Who will have all men to be saved, and to come unto the knowledge of the truth."*

When you love someone unconditionally ... you have a concern for their well-being and their future. <u>You're continually thinking about them and what's good for them</u>.

Psalm 40:17 in The Living Bible says:

> *"I am poor and weak, yet the Lord is thinking about me right now!"*

3. The world ... the greatest distance

Hebrews 11:3 in the Amplified Bible says:

> *"By faith we understand that the worlds [during the successive ages] were framed (fashioned, put in order, and equipped for their intended purpose) by the word of God, so that what we see was not made out of things which are visible."*

4. That He gave … the greatest single act

The greatest gift is never free. It always cost something that is precious to you. *People say that salvation is free … that's not true.*

Yes, it was a gift to us but it cost a great price. <u>God gave what was most precious to Him and that makes it the greatest gift of all</u>.

5. His only begotten Son … the greatest gift

<u>You can have a 2019 Audi A-8 sitting in your driveway but if you don't receive the keys, then that luxury car will never move</u>.

While Jesus willingly died for our sins … the fact is *you must accept Him as the Lord of your life to make your salvation a reality.*

6. That whosoever … the greatest opportunity

<u>You are a whosoever … I'm a whosoever … everybody you know is a whosoever</u>. We have the opportunity to accept Jesus as our Lord and turn our entire lives around "just like that" (snap your fingers).

<u>There are way too many people looking for opportunities in the wrong places</u> … Publisher's Clearinghouse or <u>*for some rich relative to pass*</u> away before they pursue their passion … the thing that is stirring in their spirit.

Joel 2:32 says:

> "And it shall come to pass, that whosoever shall call on the name of the LORD shall be delivered: for in mount Zion and in Jerusalem shall be deliverance, as the LORD hath said, and in the remnant whom the LORD shall call."

If you call on the name of the Lord ... you will be delivered.

7. Believeth ... the greatest act of faith

Hebrews 11:1 in the Amplified Bible says:

> "NOW FAITH is the assurance (the confirmation, the title deed) of the things [we] hope for, being the proof of things [we] do not see and the conviction of their reality [faith perceiving as real fact what is not revealed to the senses]."

Faith is believing in a God that you cannot see with an expectation of spending eternity in a place promised but not plotted on MapQuest. John 20:29 says:

> "Jesus saith unto him, Thomas, because thou hast seen me, thou hast believed: blessed are they that have not seen, and yet have believed."

8. In Him ... the greatest attraction

I strongly recommend you go to YouTube.com and search for, **"That's My King, Do You Know Him," by**

Dr. S. M. Lockridge, or you can Google the same name. In this powerful message, Dr. Lockridge shares in a most eloquent way why Jesus is the greatest attraction … spoken of in John 3:16.

> *My King was born King.*
> *The Bible says He's a Seven Way King.*
> *He's the King of the Jews – that's a racial King.*
> *He's the King of Israel – that's a National King.*
> *He's the King of righteousness.*
> *He's the King of the ages.*
> *He's the King of Heaven.*
> *He's the King of glory.*
> *He's the King of kings and He is the Lord of lords. Now that's my King.*
> *Well I wonder if you know Him. Do you know Him?*
> *Don't try to mislead me.*
> *Do you know my King?...*
> *No barriers can hinder Him from pouring out His blessing.*
> *Well, well, He's enduringly strong.*
> *He's entirely sincere. He's eternally steadfast.*
> *He's immortally graceful.*
> *He's imperially powerful.*
> *He's impartially merciful. That's my King.*
> *He's God's Son.*
> *He's the sinner's saviour.*
> *He's the centrepiece of civilization ….*

9. Should not perish … greatest promise

The greatest promise ever made … if you accept Jesus as your Savior … you will not go to hell. Trusting in Him will keep you from perishing in an eternal lake of fire.

It's a simple fact … if you accept Jesus … you get abundant life now and eternal life forever.

If you fail to accept Jesus as your Savior … then you will perish in torment for ever more.

It is such a <u>simple choice of gain over loss</u> but so many fail to see it.

10.   But … the greatest difference

The word "but" is the difference maker between spending eternity in hell or having everlasting life in heaven. <u>"But" is a decision every person must make that determines their destiny</u>.

Malachi 3:18 in the New Living Translation says:

> *"Then you will again see the difference between the righteous and the wicked, between those who serve God and those who do not."*

11.   Have … the greatest assurance

When you "have" accepted Jesus as the Lord of your life … you "have" the confidence … <u>the assurance in knowing that your eternal destination is secured</u> … your ticket to heaven has been paid for by the blood of Jesus and your proclamation of faith.

Like the song says, "Blessed Assurance, Jesus is mine." <u>With Him</u> you "have" this assurance **and nobody can take it away from you.**

12. Everlasting life ... the greatest future possession

In John 14:1-4 the Message Bible Jesus says:

> "Don't let this throw you. You trust God, don't you? Trust me. There is plenty of room for you in my Father's home. If that weren't so, would I have told you that I'm on my way to get a room ready for you? And if I'm on my way to get your room ready, I'll come back and get you so you can live where I live. And you already know the road I'm taking."

That's what I call 12 very good reasons to make John 3:16 the greatest scripture of all.

Day 3

Seven Ways to Get Rid of the Scum

If I were to say the word scum ... what would come to your mind?

As a boy ... the word scum would apply to *what you would find on top of stagnant water. Stagnation happens where there is no fresh movement.*

Over the years the word scum has been assigned to a person *void of a moral or ethical code*. Most often the word is used in a derogatory *manner about a person or group of people*.

So where does the word scum come from?

Proverbs 25:4-5 in the New International Version says:

> "Remove the dross from the silver, and out comes material for the silversmith; remove the wicked from the king's presence, and his throne will be established through righteousness."

According to the World English Dictionary the word dross means:

> **"the scum formed on the surface of molten metals, worthless matter and waste."**

Here Are the "Seven Reasons to Get Rid of the Scum in Your Life."

1. Recognize scum is holding you back.

If you find yourself living with or tolerating less than the best ... *then identify the scum that is holding you back.*

If you continue to allow dross ... or the scum of relationships to dominate your conversations or *what you do or don't do ... then you're allowing scum to hold you back.*

If you fail to take a risk ... *to passionately pursue your dreams because of what others say and/or do ...* then you're allowing the scum to hold you back.

2. Identify the Scum.

Matthew 7:20 in the New Living Translation says:

> *"Yes, just as you can identify a tree by its fruit, so you can identify people by their actions."*

You can identify a true believer ... by the fruit of his or her labor.

You can identify a true friend ... by their presence or *the lack thereof when you face a personal crisis*.

You can identify negative ... *unbelieving* ... faithless people ... by the fruit of their lips.

According to the scripture ... *you and I will avoid the scum in our lives by becoming fruit inspectors*.

Matthew 7:16 in the New Living Translation says:

> *"You can identify them by their fruit, that is, by the way they act. Can you pick grapes from thorn bushes, or figs from thistles?"*

Let me repeat that:

> *"You can identify them by their fruit, that is, by the way they act."*

In case you didn't get it:

> *"You can identify them by their fruit, that is, by the way they act."*

3. Separate Yourself from The Scum.

Psalm 119:119 in the New Living Translation says:

> *"You skim off the wicked of the earth like scum;*

no wonder I love to obey your laws!"

Scripturally speaking, *we not only shouldn't allow the scum (anything not of God) into our thought process … we shouldn't even allow them into our house!*

2 John 1:10 in the Amplified Bible says:

> *"If anyone comes to you and does not bring this doctrine [is disloyal to what Jesus Christ taught], do not receive him [do not accept him, do not welcome or admit him] into [your] house or bid him Godspeed or give him any encouragement."*

4. Replace the Scum with Purity toward God.

Malachi 3:2-4 in The Living Bible says:

> *"But who can live when he appears? Who can endure his coming? For he is like a blazing fire refining precious metal, and he can bleach the dirtiest garments! Like a refiner of silver he will sit and closely watch as the dross is burned away. He will purify the Levites, the ministers of God, refining them like gold or silver, so that they will do their work for God with pure hearts."*

There was a time in my life when I thought I had a lot of friends.

Why did I think that? *Because they said they were my*

friends. However, when we went through a particularly tough time in our lives … I looked around and found that a good many of those "friends" were mere acquaintances and *they disappeared when the heat of the enemy's attack was directed at my life.*

When the heat is applied … *those previously-thought friends will clear away like the dross … the scum* and *leave you with friends who are the real silver and gold.*

Sometimes your circumstances may remove the scum … other times *it might require a deliberate decision on your part* … either way, you're the better for it.

5. Value Increases When Scum Is Removed.

Any time you remove any impediments or scum from your life … then the value increases. That is just as true in life as it is in precious metals.

Proverbs 25:4-5 in The Living Bible says:

> "When you remove dross from silver, you have sterling ready for the silversmith. When you remove corrupt men from the king's court, his reign will be just and fair."

If you have real "silver" ware or sterling silverware, *then you know it needs to be polished on a somewhat regular basis … to keep it looking pure and shiny.* However, if you don't keep it clean … then the ap-

pearance of the scum will tarnish the perceived value of the silver.

You will also notice the scripture makes it clear that things will be better in the King's Court when the scum is removed.

You are the Child of a King ... *when you remove the dross ... the scum impacting your life ...* then you will be of greater value to the King of Kings.

6. Everyone Is Blessed When Scum Removed.

When impurities are removed out of your thought life, *your personal habits and your friendships ...* then everything is purer and of greater value.

When you remove what's been holding you back from doing the things God has called you to do ... *then you and everyone around you will be blessed ... simply because you're in the center of God's perfect will for your life.*

Malachi 3:2-4 in the New International Version says:

> *"But who can endure the day of his coming? Who can stand when he appears? For he will be like a refiner's fire or a launderer's soap. He will sit as a refiner and purifier of silver; he will purify the Levites and refine them like gold and silver. Then the Lord will have men who will bring offer-*

ings in righteousness, and the offerings of Judah and Jerusalem will be acceptable to the Lord, as in days gone by, as in former years."

When you're pure before God … you will bring offerings that will be a blessing to others, financially and otherwise.

7. Your Usefulness to God Increases When Scum is removed.

When you remove the scum … and become pure … you and God will get closer.

Proverbs 22:11 in the New Living Translation says:

"Whoever loves a pure heart and gracious speech will have the king as a friend."

When you remove the scum … and become pure … God will bless you.

Matthew 5:8 in the New Living Translation says:

"God blesses those whose hearts are pure, for they will see God."

Two final thoughts on the benefits of removing the scum from your life:

First, the washing of the water of the Word will

remove the scum from your life and give you a pure heart.

1 Timothy 1:5 in the New Living Translation says:

> *"The purpose of my instruction is that all believers would be filled with love that comes from a pure heart, a clear conscience, and genuine faith."*

Second, if you want to be in His presence, then you must do whatever is necessary to rid yourself of the scum … as you embrace the pure, the powerful and the positive from the Word of God.

2 Timothy 2:22 in the New Living Translation says:

> "Run from anything that stimulates youthful lusts. Instead, pursue righteous living, faithfulness, love, and peace. Enjoy the companionship of those who call on the Lord with pure hearts."

In other words … it's time to get rid of the dross … the scum … so you can walk in a new level of revelation.

The last part of Luke 4:18 in the Message Bible which you're going to love … says:

> *"… To set the burdened and battered free, to announce, 'This is God's year to act!'"*

Day 4

8 Things I Will Always Remember

Psalm 119:93 in the Amplified Bible says:

> *"I will never forget Your precepts, [how can I?] for it is by them You have quickened me (granted me life)."*

If you're drawing a breath as you hear these words, then you have been granted life. And truly, not just life … but life eternal … abundant … good life.

John 10:10 in the New Living Translation says:

> *"The thief's purpose is to steal and kill and destroy. My purpose is to give them a rich and satisfying life."*

What is a rich and satisfying life?

As I asked several days ago … is it living from paycheck to paycheck … a rich and satisfying life? Absolutely Not.

Is wondering where your next meal *is coming from* …

a rich and satisfying life? Hardly.

Is wondering where your children are *and worrying about the kinds of things they're doing* ... a rich and satisfying life? Certainly not.

Is spending more time in a doctor's office or *being sick* the standard for a rich and satisfying life? No way.

A rich and satisfying life ... is living humbly before God ... studying His Word ... *being in His presence while walking in His prosperity and your inheritance as a child of the King* ... and yes, *manifesting His precious promises in your life.*

That's the kind of life that God wants to grant us ... *but it is conditional upon our never forgetting His precepts*. It is through our obedience to His Word that we receive the manifestation of everything He has in store for us.

Psalm 119:92 in the Message Bible says:

> *"If your revelation hadn't delighted me so, I would have given up when the hard times came."*

The revelation of God's Word in your life ... will take you through whatever hard times you may be facing.

Your success in life is not an accident but a consequence of the decisions you make and the actions you take based on the Word of God.

Following His precepts ... *obeying His instructions is not just for emergencies ... it is a daily function that should never become routine* ... as His Word is a fresh as every morning dew.

The Living Bible Translation of Psalm 119:92-99 offers eight profound life-changing insights into the things that we should always remember *and thus never ever forget.*

Verse 92:

"I would have despaired and perished unless your laws had been my deepest delight."

In verse 92 we learn that our deepest delight should be His Word and *its instructions for daily living.* It's the only guaranteed way to overcome adversity and personal distress.

Verse 93:

"I will never lay aside your laws, for you have used them to restore my joy and health."

In verse 93 we are guaranteed that obeying His commands will restore our joy and our health.

Nothing you can buy in any store in any mall *could ever guarantee the restoration of your joy* ... but the Word of God does. *Things will never heal a hurt or restore your joy but the Word of God can.*

There is no physician or medical facility in the world that can guarantee the restoration of your health ... but the Word of God does.

Verse 94:

> "I am yours! Save me! For I have tried to live according to your desires."

In times of adversity ... you have been given the right to call upon Him to save you from every attack ... simply because you have been living according to His instructions.

Exodus 23:22 says:

> "But if you will indeed listen to and obey His voice ... I will be an enemy to your enemies and an adversary to your adversaries."

Psalm 118:6 in the Message Bible says:

> "God's now at my side and I'm not afraid; who would dare lay a hand on me?"

If there is ever a verse that should comfort you ... it's this verse. Talk about comfort and confidence in the midst of every battle and attack.

You have a personal defense system stronger, more powerful and accurate than any natural weapon. The Pentagon only wishes they could send soldiers into battle with the assurance of victory that only the Word can give.

Verse 95:

"Though the wicked hide along the way to kill me, I will quietly keep my mind upon your promises."

You can also receive peace and comfort in the following two verses.

First, Isaiah 54:17 in the Amplified Bible says:

"But no weapon that is formed against you shall prosper, and every tongue that shall rise against you in judgment you shall show to be in the wrong. This [peace, righteousness, security, triumph over opposition] is the heritage of the servants of the Lord [those in whom the ideal Servant of the Lord is reproduced]; this is the righteousness or the vindication which they obtain from Me [this is that which I impart to them as their justification], says the Lord."

Second, Hebrews 13:5-6 in the Amplified Bible says:

"So we take comfort and are encouraged and confidently and boldly say, The Lord is my Helper; I will not be seized with alarm [I will not fear or dread or be terrified]. What can man do to me?"

Your peace, comfort and protection is a done deal.

God says so!

Verse 96:

> "Nothing is perfect except your words."

As powerful as the Declaration of Independence, the Magna Carta and the Gettysburg Address are … there is nothing as perfect as the Word of God.

All 800,000 words are perfect … the right word in the right sentence in the right sequence.

2 Samuel 22:31 in The Living Bible says:

> "As for God, his way is perfect; The word of the Lord is true. He shields all who hide behind him."

God clearly wants us to understand that His way … what we think … is perfect.

He wants us to know and fully understand that His Word is true. That's why the exact wording of 2 Samuel 22:31 is repeated in Psalm 18:30.

Verse 97:

> "Oh, how I love them. I think about them all day long."

We should be thinking of His Word every minute of every day. It is our daily guide for learning and living according to His instructions.

Job 23:12 in the New Living Translation says:

> "I have not departed from his commands, but have treasured his words more than daily food."

His Word … His instructions are to treasured even more than the food we eat.

Verse 98:

> "They make me wiser than my enemies because they are my constant guide."

Psalm 119:133 in the New Living Translation says:

> "Guide my steps by your word, so I will not be overcome by evil."

James 3:13 in the New Living Translation says:

> "If you are wise and understand God's ways, prove it by living an honorable life, doing good works with the humility that comes from wisdom."

Verse 99:

> "Yes, wiser than my teachers, for I am ever thinking of your rules."

Psalm 77:12-14 in The Living Bible says:

> "Those wonderful deeds are constantly in my

thoughts. I cannot stop thinking about them. O God, your ways are holy. Where is there any other as mighty as you? You are the God of miracles and wonders! You still demonstrate your awesome power."

You have just received eight scriptural reasons from Psalm 119 as to why you should never forget His Word … so you can experience a rich and satisfying life.

Day 5

If You're Doing It ... Stop It

How many of you have children?

Have you ever **written instructions for your kids to follow** ... **only to have them ignored?**

Have you *ever told your kids something only to have them forget and suffer the consequences of their temporary memory lapse*?

Were your instructions either written or verbal words of wisdom that, *if followed*, would have *saved your children* from *experiencing* anxiety, heartache, embarrassment, pain or loss?

Why do you think your children **didn't listen**, *obey* and/or *learn from your instructions?*

Do you think **they weren't really listening**?

Do you think they *weren't paying attention?*

Do you think they **weren't able to read and compre-**

hend your instructions?

Do you think they **doubted your words of wisdom**?

Do you think **they thought they knew more than you**?

Do you think they *just didn't take the time necessary to follow your advice?*

Do you think they **were just being disobedient**?

Do you think *they just didn't care?*

Did the fact that your children didn't follow your instructions <u>make you want to give up on them</u> or stop giving them the benefit of your counsel?

I doubt it.

Now let's bring this question home.

When you're told something by an expert ... *do you always believe it?*

Do you always take his/her advice?

If not, why not? Have you ever thought about that?

How many times do we have to hear something to realize that it's true?

How many times do you have **to read something**

penned by the world's foremost expert to believe what He says? Or **do what He asks**?

How many times do you have **to read something in the Word of God to know that He says what He means and means what He says**?

How many times will you ignore His instructions that *could save you anxiety,* **heartache***, embarrassment, pain or loss?*

How can we expect our earthly children to do something that we're sometimes unwilling to do for our Heavenly Father … like just follow His instructions?

If God tells us to "be not afraid" … **how many times does He have to tell us something before we get it and live it?**

We are told **26 times** in the **King James Version** of the Bible to "be not afraid."

There are **44 verses** in the **Message Bible** that say, **"Don't be afraid,"** and **66 verses** in the *New Living Translation* with the exact same scriptural directive for us.

Regardless of whether you say *"Be not afraid"* or *"Don't be afraid"* the message is clear … yet way too many believers are afraid.

Afraid of what will happen **if they lose their job**.

Afraid of what will happen if their *unfaithful spouse leaves them*.

Afraid of the **bad report the doctor gave them**.

Afraid *of losing a child when you require them to follow the rules of your house*.

Afraid of **losing your retirement income**.

Afraid of *being evicted from your apartment*.

Afraid of your *supervisor at work*.

Afraid of **what you'll do if your house goes into foreclosure**.

Afraid of *dropping sales in your business*.

Afraid of **what's happening in the world's political and economic system**.

Afraid of any and everything.

I think you're getting the picture.

"But yes, Brother Harold, it's easy to say 'be not afraid' unless you're the one going through the fire."

You know, in reading the Bible, **I've never seen an * (asterisk)** that says this scripture *doesn't apply to certain people going through this battle*, that situation, problem or circumstance.

I believe that every word in the scripture ... all 800,000 of them were *carefully chosen just for us as we travel through this life.*

1. You have the word from the ultimate authority.

"... But he saith unto them, It is I; **be not afraid.***"*

— John 6:20 —

2. The creator of heaven and earth *has specific words* for you.

"... ***be not afraid of them****: for the LORD thy God is with thee ..."*

— Deuteronomy 20:1 —

3. You don't have to be afraid *because you're not the one fighting the battle.*

"... Thus saith the LORD unto you, ***Be not afraid*** *nor dismayed by reason of this great multitude; for the battle is not yours, but God's."*

— 2 Chronicles 20:15 —

4. There are *more fighters on your team than on* anybody else's.

"... Be strong and courageous, ***be not afraid*** *nor dismayed for the king of Assyria, nor for all the multitude that is with him: for there be more*

with us than with him."

— 2 Chronicles 32:7 —

5. The leader of your team has *guaranteed a quick victory.*

"And the LORD said unto Joshua, **Be not afraid** because of them: for tomorrow about this time will I deliver them up all slain before Israel ..."

— Joshua 11:6 —

6. No matter, where you live or what you're doing ... your team leader is always with you.

"Have not I commanded thee? Be strong and of a good courage; **be not afraid**, neither be thou dismayed: for the LORD thy God is with thee whithersoever thou goest."

— Joshua 1:9 —

7. You don't have to be *afraid of what you see.*

"... **Be not afraid**: for what sawest thou? ..."

— 1 Samuel 28:13 —

8. You don't have to be *afraid of what you've heard.*

"... Be not afraid of the words which thou hast heard ..."

— *2 Kings 19:6* —

9. You don't have to be *afraid of secret attacks by the enemy.*

> "… **Be not afraid** of sudden fear, neither of the desolation of the wicked, when it cometh."

— *Proverbs 3:25* —

10. You don't have to be afraid *because your enemy can't harm you.*

> "… **Be not afraid** of them; for they cannot do evil …"

— *Jeremiah 10:5* —

11. You will be *delivered from the attacks of the enemy.*

> "… be not afraid of him, saith the LORD: for I am with you to save you, and to deliver you from his hand."

— *Jeremiah 42:11* —

12. You *don't have to be afraid of what "they" say about you.*

> "And thou, son of man, **be not afraid** of them, neither be afraid of their words, though briers

*and thorns be with thee, and thou dost dwell among scorpions: **be not afraid** of their words, nor be dismayed at their looks, though they be a rebellious house."*

— Ezekiel 2:6 —

The Word of God also gives you some **very specific instructions on what to do to keep from being afraid**.

First, you must believe the Word of God.

*"… **Be not afraid**, only believe."*

— Mark 5:36 —

Second, you must be *cheerful in the midst of an attack*.

*"… Be of good cheer; it is I; **be not afraid**."*

— Matthew 14:27 —

Third, once you've energized your faith, you must GET UP and *fulfill God's assignment for your life*.

*"And Jesus came and touched them, and said, Arise, and **be not afraid**."*

— Matthew 17:7 —

Fourth, just as God has delivered you … you must

testify to others about God's Word so they experience His manifestation in their own lives too.

> *"Then said Jesus unto them, Be not afraid: go tell my brethren that they go into Galilee, and there shall they see me."*
>
> *— Matthew 28:10 —*

Fifth, you must Praise the Lord continually … *confident in the knowledge that no man or "no thing" can harm you.*

> *"In God, whose word I praise, in God I trust; I will **not be afraid**. What can mortal man do to me?"*
>
> *— Psalm 56:4 NIV —*

Sixth, your reward for not being afraid will come from a source with unlimited benefits.

> *"After all these things, this word of God came to Abram in a vision: '**Don't be afraid**, Abram. I'm your shield. Your reward will be grand!'"*
>
> *— Genesis 15:1 MSG —*

Did this teaching witness to your spirit … if not … read and re-read it again and again until you get it into your spirit. *God has instructed you to BE NOT AFRAID.*

RichThoughts for Breakfast Volume 6

Day 6

3 Things to Know in Battle

As I was pondering yesterday's teaching ... on how God instructs us not be afraid ... I was led to Habakkuk 3:19 which I've read probably dozens and dozens of times:

> *"The LORD God is my strength, and he will make my feet like hinds' feet, and he will make me to walk upon mine high places ..."*

But recently I read Habakkuk 3:19 for the first time in the Amplified Bible translation where it says:

> *"The Lord God is my Strength, my personal bravery, and my invincible army; He makes my feet like hinds' feet and will make me to walk [not to stand still in terror, but to walk] and make [spiritual] progress upon my high places [of trouble, suffering, or responsibility]! ..."*

My real strength ... **is not the result of a workout regimen at the gym** ... because that will not last.

My real strength ... is not in my cash reserves or my

investment portfolio … because it can be here today and gone tomorrow.

My real strength … **is not in my family and friends** … because people change and they pass into eternity.

My real strength … ***is not in what I know*** … <u>**because unless I have an intimate knowledge of Him**</u>**, I will know nothing of real and lasting value**.

My real strength … **in every challenge and opportunity I face** … is ***the confident knowledge that God will never leave me or forsake me*** (Hebrews 13:8).

I will **never cower in the face of adversity or overwhelming odds** … because His strength makes me brave.

I am empowered in battle … **strengthened with His presence and power**.

Psalm 18:29 says:

> *"For by thee I have run through a troop; and by my God have I leaped over a wall."*

Psalm 18:29 in the New Living Translation says:

> *"In your strength I can crush an army; with my God I can scale any wall."*

I need never fear any enemy attack … because <u>He is my invincible army</u>.

When things around are falling apart … *when it seems that I'm being attacked on every side* … **I do not have to be afraid, feel or face terror** … because *the Lord God is my strength, protector, defender and deliverer*.

Isaiah 54:17 says:

> *"No weapon that is formed against thee shall prosper; and every tongue that shall rise against thee in judgment thou shalt condemn. This is the heritage of the servants of the LORD, and their righteousness is of me, saith the LORD."*

If there is one thing that you want to know in the midst of an attack … *it's that you're making progress* … that you're headed to victory.

Romans 8:27 says:

> *"Yet in all these things we are more than conquerors through Him who loved us."*

In every battle that I face … *the things that I want most of all is to feel His presence and be comforted, strengthened and encouraged by His Word*.

Romans 8:31 says:

> *"What shall we then say to these things? If God*

be for us, who can be against us?"

If you've ever endured an enemy blitzkrieg, you know the peace you find in His Word.

I remember during one particularly difficult period of our lives … a dear friend gave us 2 Corinthians 4:8-9.

> *"We are troubled on every side, yet not distressed; we are perplexed, but not in despair; Persecuted, but not forsaken; cast down, but not destroyed."*

As I read that verse … I felt that I had been thrown a lifeline.

The Message Bible translation of 2 Corinthians 4:8-9 says it this way:

> *"We've been surrounded and battered by troubles, but we're not demoralized; we're not sure what to do, but we know that God knows what to do; we've been spiritually terrorized, but God hasn't left our side; we've been thrown down, but we haven't broken."*

Several days ago, I mentioned that one of the **most successful military strategies an enemy can employ in warfare is to separate you from your supply lines** … ***to keep you from receiving reinforcements or supplies***.

That's exactly what the devil wants to do when he has you, your family, your finances and/or your health under attack … **he wants to separate you from your supply line** … **to keep you from receiving reinforcements and orders from your spiritual headquarters.**

The only way the enemy can spiritually terrorize you … *is by doubt, separation and isolation.*

When you find yourself under attack <u>whether it's a natural enemy or spiritual enemy</u> indecision can be costly. Even though you may not know the best strategy to employ at any given moment … God does.

As the verse said, *"… we're not sure what to do, we know God knows what to do …"*

There are **three things that you should know in every battle**.

The first is found in Deuteronomy 31:6 in the Message Bible which says:

> *"God is striding ahead of you. He's right there with you. He won't let you down; he won't leave you. Don't be intimidated. Don't worry."*

You don't have to be intimated by trouble or spiritual terrorism … God is right there with you and *will NEVER let you down and He will NEVER leave you.*

The scripture says, *"Don't Worry."*

It doesn't say … **"you can worry if you want to."**

It doesn't say … *"you can worry in specific circumstances."*

It doesn't say … **"you can worry some of the time."**

No, you and I are told … **DON'T WORRY**.

<u>The second thing you need to know is found in Proverbs 3:5-6 (MSB)</u>:

> *"Trust God from the bottom of your heart; don't try to figure out everything on your own. Listen for God's voice in everything you do, everywhere you go; he's the one who will keep you on track."*

The part of the verse that says *"… **don't try to figure out everything on your own** …"* is **critically important to your emotional, physical and spiritual well-being**.

If you're trying to figure things out … **to solve your problems by yourself** … <u>then you don't need God</u>.

Simply said, <u>***only one of you will be working on and through the problem, situation or attack***</u> … **that's either you or Him**.

*As the verse says, you must "… **listen for God's voice in everything you do** …"*

I have found that **when facing life's challenges ... there are multiple voices vying for your attention.**

Everybody has an opinion on what you should and shouldn't be doing. *How you should and shouldn't be responding.* But yet, **there is only one voice that you're told to listen for ... His voice.**

The reason you listen for His voice ... *is because He's the one that will "... **keep you on track**."*

The third thing you should do in battle is found in Isaiah 48:17:

> "Thus saith the LORD, thy Redeemer, the Holy One of Israel; I am the LORD thy God which teacheth thee to profit, which leadeth thee by the way that thou shouldest go."

Not only should you not worry and listen for His voice ... *but realize that He's the only One who will teach you to profit in every situation.*

According to Strong's Concordance the word profit is the Hebrew word ya`al (ya el) (H3276) which means to:

"gain, benefit, profit."

Child of God, *be encouraged when you follow His divine direction* ... **He will sustain you through every attack** and *even cause you to "gain, benefit and profit" from the attacks of the enemy.*

But you and I must follow His direction. We must understand and obey the words found in Isaiah 48:17 in the Message Bible which says:

> *"I am God, your God, who teaches you how to live right and well. I show you what to do, where to go."*

It's comforting to know that God will cause you to live right and well … that He will show you what to do and where to go … to overcome and profit from every attack of the enemy.

And we all say, "Hallelujah, Thank You, Jesus."

Day 7

It's Your Character, Not Your Checkbook Balance

Being rich does not make a person evil.

I'm continually amazed at *how many well-meaning Christians think that being rich and being evil are synonymous*. How do they explain Abraham, Isaac and Jacob?

Oftentimes, they cite Proverbs 28:6 as *a justification for their "poverty is good" ... "rich is bad" theology*. The scripture says:

> "Better is the poor that walketh in his uprightness, than he that is perverse in his ways, though he be rich."

If you read this scripture accurately ... <u>you will see that it's the perverseness that is being condemned and not the fact that they might be rich</u>.

The verse is condemning those who are perverse in their ways "even though" they may be rich. *It is saying: don't let a perverse person off the hook "just be-*

cause" they are rich.

The word perverse is the Hebrew word `iqqesh (H6141) and it means:

"twisted, distorted, crooked, perverse, perverted."

In other words, **a perverse person is a wicked person**. However, *nowhere in the definition of the word perverse do you find the words "wealthy" or "rich" included*.

However, it does not exclude that fact that *the words that make up the definition of perverse could also include a rich person … but it could just as easily reference someone who's so broke they can't pick up all the pieces.*

The idea that being rich was evil and being poor was Godly originated after the death of Alexander the Great.

There were orders of monks that rose up who took vows of poverty. *They were viewed by some others as super spiritual because of this vow.*

The reality is that many so-called religious leaders did not want Christians following the teachings of Christ when it came to money. **If people are poor they become dependent upon those who are educated and have money.**

<u>For centuries it was against the law to own a Bible because *it kept the people dependent upon the rulers who controlled the church*</u>.

In the 1380s, John Wycliffe was instrumental in making copies of Bibles in a person's language because the church was not preaching the whole Bible.

The theology that to be poor meant you were Godly *originated as a desire to control rather than deliver the children of God.*

My purpose in this teaching is not to make this an in-depth teaching on how prosperity was minimized, *if not condemned*, on the basis of scriptural interpretation. Perhaps that will become a teaching another time, if and when God directs.

Point of fact, Proverbs 28:6 offers a fairly balanced scriptural view of the poor and rich. Please get a hold of this next statement. <u>**It's not your economic station in life that counts but rather your character before God**</u>.

Let me say this as clearly as I know how.

Money can't buy character and Godly behavior but it certainly can corrupt it. *<u>Poverty is not a litmus test for Godliness nor does it guarantee it</u>.* <u>Poverty in the final analysis should develop a dependence on God without using it as a justification for failure</u>.

Make no mistake about it … *the Bible has just as*

many examples of the righteous rich as it does the wicked rich.

I taught it for years ... but it bears repeating. *Money is a magnifier ... it just reveals what's already in your character.*

Money is neutral ... *by itself it does nothing.*

If a person who is a church-goer suddenly comes into a large amount of money and *he then chooses to spend his Sundays out in his new boat, his character reveals who he really was* ... just a church-goer.

However, if a person who is a church-goer suddenly comes into a large amount of money and he chooses to remain a committed part of his church, *his character reveals that his heart was truly after the things of God*.

Money merely reflects what lives inside a person ... and money will definitely reveal it.

Now let's get back to Proverbs 28:6 which in the Amplified Bible says:

> "Better is the poor man who walks in his integrity than he who willfully goes in double and wrong ways, though he is rich."

Notice the last part of the verse where is says "... though he is rich." <u>The scripture is a condemnation of wickedness, not wealth</u>. It's not the fact that a person is rich but the wickedness of their heart that is the focus of this verse. **Money brings out who people are … on the inside.**

The verse does say that it's better to be poor. *It says it's better to see a poor person who walks in integrity than to see a rich person who is evil*.

It's the character of a person's heart and not the balance in their checkbook or lack thereof that determines who they are.

Two other things, I feel led to discuss.

First, a few days ago, I made the following post on my social media account:

> "Make no mistake about it! God is interested in your finances. If He wasn't interested then it would be ridiculous for 20% of the scriptures to deal with money, wealth, finances, property, lands, possessions, tithes and giving. And yet they do. Psalm 35:27 tells us, … yea, let them say continually, Let the Lord be magnified, which hath pleasure in the prosperity of His servants.'"

There was one person who follows me that took exception to this post.

He wrote, in part, the following:

> "Money unfortunately has become a major distraction in our church today. The ones that have

it will do anything to keep it and the ones that don't have it dream about getting it … God gives us everything we need. When u mention the rich giving up worldly possessions to redistribute the wealth evenly to eliminate poverty, they label that Socialism or Communism. I call it True Christianity."

So, in response, I posted the following:

"… we're blessed to be a blessing … no question about that … you can't bless anybody or help spread the gospel if you're broke … never presuppose that because people are rich that the gospel isn't their first priority … and for the record, redistribution of wealth is unscriptural and morally wrong."

I have a revelation … money is not a distraction in the church … *money may reveal the problem* **… if it shows a person's real character, but money itself is not the problem.**

Money in the church is why we can send missionaries to spread the gospel or send young people to church camp when their parents can't afford it. *Money allows the pastor to rest because the church can afford to hire someone to clean the bathrooms at the church.*

Money buys electricity and heat in the winter and air conditioning in the summer *so people are not distracted and can hear the Word preached.* Money provides a *food pantry and clothing program for the disabled, abused, sick and those who've lost their jobs.*

Choosing to take the high road and upon the advice of my fine wife … I stopped the exchange with the following post.

> "I disagree with your basic premise and your assumptions … the Word doesn't talk about redistribution of wealth … it talks about giving … tithes and offerings … I wish you well …."

And just for the record, **redistribution of wealth is anything but Christian**. *Whether redistribution of wealth is a socialistic or communistic doctrine is irrelevant to me because it's unscriptural.* Perhaps I'll teach on that another day.

Here's the final point I want to make:

Never ever stereotype someone based on their net worth. **People with a heart for the things of God can be found in every tax bracket and income level.** *It's a person's character … not their investment portfolio that determines their priorities in life*.

Acts 10:35 in the Amplified Bible says:

> "But in every nation he who venerates and has a reverential fear for God, treating Him with worshipful obedience and living uprightly, is acceptable to Him and sure of being received and welcomed [by Him]."

As this verse explains, **character is not based on money … it is based on the contents of our hearts before God**.

Day 8

Don't Say That

As I read the letter of one precious lady ... God stirred me to teach about part of *what she wrote on her prayer request reply.* She quoted part of the verse found in Acts 3:6.

> *"... Silver and gold have I none; but such as I have give I thee ..."*

The lady wanted me to pray for her to have a financial harvest *even though she wasn't sowing a seed.* She quoted part of the scripture as a justification. It's one that preachers who don't believe in prosperity *use to spiritualize their beliefs.*

Let me share eight things that I know with absolute certainty.

1. I know that people are hurting because there is an economic famine in this land.

2. I know that everything reproduces after its own kind. (Genesis 1:12)

3. I know that I pray for as many people who don't

give to the Debt Free Army as I do for those who sow their precious seeds into this ministry.

4. I know this sweet lady thinks prayer is all she can sow at this time.

5. I know this dear saint doesn't understand the spiritual implications of saying, "This is all I have," or <u>she would never be saying it</u>.

6. I know that way too many believers are looking at what they don't have *instead of what they do have*.

7. I know that while prayer is powerful and desirable it will not produce a Harvest. Reaping without a seed being sown is not possible *because it violates God's principles of sowing and reaping*.

8. Finally, I know that this lady and sadly, too many other folks, <u>don't really understand the fullness of what Acts 3:6 is saying</u>.

"Then Peter said, Silver and gold have I none; but such as I have give I thee: In the name of Jesus Christ of Nazareth rise up and walk."

I want to focus on the word have which is the Greek word echō (G2192) and according to the Strong's Concordance is defined as:

"1) to have, i.e. to hold; 2) to have i.e.

own, possess; external things such as pertain to property or riches or furniture or utensils or goods or food etc."

Peter was talking about what he had "at the moment." He was discussing what he had available to him *at the time he was walking by this man in need* because he knew … *he was confident that God was about to do something supernatural … beyond material need.*

Peter also knew this man was looking for someone to put food on his table for a day.

Acts 3:5 says:

> *"And he gave heed unto them, expecting to receive something of them."*

This man was clearly looking to someone to meet His need for a day … *to give him his daily bread.*

Instead *Peter was teaching this man a spiritual truth.*

When you look to people to meet your needs for a day … that's all you're going to get.

There are way too many believers who are living from day to day *because they're looking for natural sources to meet their needs.*

What Peter gave to this man was *the miracle-working power of God.*

This was a defining moment in this man's life. *He was about to change his old way of thinking … his old way of doing things … his tradition of begging for food from day to day forever.*

Each of us needs a defining moment in our lives … *when we stop living day to day and begin moving in God's miracle working power, where there is never a question as to whether or not our needs will be met.*

I'm sure that the amount of money this lame man received each day could be affected by circumstances … *the local economy … by the weather* and *how quickly people ran into the synagogue when they were late.*

This man was totally dependent upon the generosity of those people *who had been blessed through their obedience to God's principles* of seedtime and harvest. The reality is that he should have already been dependent upon Jehovah Jireh, His Provider.

The implication of many well-meaning folks is that Peter had nothing to give him because he was broke. I don't want to spend a lot of time on this but *Peter was anything but broke.*

In a time when very few people owned their own business … Peter did. *He was a fisherman who had his own boat … he had his own crew.* Not only that, *the scripture reveals that his family had servants.*

Does that sound like a broke man to you? I don't think so.

Peter was simply trying to help this man look beyond his current level of expectation.

Two scriptures come to mind.

First, Psalm 5:3 in the New Living Translation says:

> *"Listen to my voice in the morning, Lord. Each morning I bring my requests to you and wait expectantly."*

The second scripture is Psalm 62:5 which says:

> *"My soul, wait thou only upon God; for my expectation is from him."*

Peter wasn't broke … *he was seeking to raise this man's level of expectation* so he could experience the miracle-working, *life-changing*, bondage-breaking, *yoke-destroying* power of God.

When we're looking to individuals to meet our needs … *we will never see that God is waiting for us to move out in faith*.

Before concluding this teaching there is one other important spiritual principle we need to discuss and understand.

I'm continually amazed and saddened by the number

of people who want me to pray for them to have a financial breakthrough without ever sowing a seed.

If you've followed my teaching at all ... you will know that God put forth a principle that is so common we take it for granted. It is the principle of seedtime and harvest. *It is as simple as the examples you experience every day.* If you don't sow ... you don't reap. It's really that simple.

The last sentence in the Amplified Bible translation of Galatians 6:7 says:

> "... For whatever a man sows, that and that only is what he will reap."

Personalized truth ... Miya, Esther, Sandra, Dwight ...

> "... For whatever <<Name>> sows, <u>that and that only</u> is what <<he/she>> will reap."

Principle # 1:

If you sow, you reap ... if you don't sow ... you won't reap.

Principle # 2:

Your words will empower or eliminate *the enemy's ability to wreak havoc in your financial life.*

The enemy is powerless to impact our lives ... until we give him the power. *It's done by how we* communicate our current financial situation with the words we speak or the things that we confirm in writing.

Make no mistake about it. The enemy wants us living in fear over the appearance of lack in our financial situations.

If the enemy can transfer fear into your mind, he immediately has the ability to take advantage over you.

If the enemy can get you to believe you have nothing to give … he has the ability to take advantage of you.

If the enemy can get you confessing lack in your life … he has the ability to take advantage of you.

If we *sow words that indicate a lack of faith in God's provision … or over his ability to move in our current situation …* then we are going to live a life of financial shortage. Life and death is in the power of our tongue (Proverbs 18:21).

If we say, *"This is all I have," then we are negating the promises of God … we are consciously or unconsciously limiting the power of God to bring financial deliverance into our lives … and giving up our right to the financial last will and testament of our Lord.*

God wants us to get our eyes on Him and His ability to create supernatural manifestation in our lives … it's time for each of us to raise our level of expectation.

Day 9

Imagine You're Living the Good Life of God

In my travels I've met a lot of people who want the blessings of God *without the relationship or the lifestyle of a believer.*

You can't live like the devil all week *then run around the church on Sunday shouting 'Shandi' … quoting 3 John 2 thinking everything is going to be all right*. <u>It doesn't work that way</u>.

God loves His children and wants us blessed *but His principles also apply*. His Word is filled with promises and blessings *but they often hold a requirement before they are fulfilled … not the least of which is to seek and serve Him with ALL our heart.*

The key word in that last sentence is "ALL" our heart. *God cannot be fooled. He knows if we really care or just show up when trouble strikes.* We can't play games with Him or hope He's not noticing *when we turn our back on Him.*

Quoting the scripture like Captain Religious or *singing like Sister Precious* is not going to open up the windows of heaven over our lives.

Our Heavenly Father gives us very clear instructions *on how we should act in order to live a life worth living.*

The key to living a Godly life is found throughout the scriptures but today I was led to Ezekiel 18:5.

> *"But if a man be just, and do that which is lawful and right …"*

Here's a question, *what is lawful in the sight of civil authorities and what is right in the sight of God?* Sometimes they are the same … and sometimes we as Christians are held to a higher standard before God.

Is stealing cable TV signals lawful?

Is cheating on your income taxes lawful?

Is driving away from a fast food restaurant with too much change the right or Godly thing to do?

Is it okay to buy things that you know you really don't need but yet it will take you years to pay for? And, yes, you bought it "right" in the sight of God?

Is stealing time or supplies from your employer lawful and right?

So the question is . . . *what is a just man?*

In the Strong's Concordance, just is defined 162 times as righteous. Strong's defines righteous as being:

"righteous in government, right in one's cause, righteous in conduct and character, as justified and vindicated by God."

<u>Reading the definition of just in Strong's Concordance</u> *<u>makes me realize that we can definitely use some</u> <u>more just (a whole lot more) men and women in our</u> <u>government</u>*.

I'm not getting into politics … but speaking from a merely moral point of view, I think you'd agree with me.

I think the Message Bible translation of *Ezekiel 18:5-9 gives you an excellent picture of what's just, righteous and required to live a full, Godly life.*

> "Imagine a person who lives well, treating others fairly, keeping good relationships—
>   doesn't eat at the pagan shrines,
>   doesn't worship the idols so popular in Israel,
>   doesn't seduce a neighbor's spouse,
>   doesn't indulge in casual sex,
>   doesn't bully anyone,
>   doesn't pile up bad debts,
>   doesn't steal,
>   doesn't refuse food to the hungry,
>   doesn't refuse clothing to the ill-clad,
>   doesn't exploit the poor,

doesn't live by impulse and greed,
doesn't treat one person better than another,
But lives by my statutes and faithfully
honors and obeys my laws.
This person who lives upright and well shall live
a full and true life. Decree of God, the Master."

As I read this *passage, the Lord said that too many of His children are eating at pagan shrines and worshiping popular idols.*

Now I'm confident that many people reading my words in this teaching are saying to themselves, *"Thank God I don't do that."*

Here's something to think about.

If the car in your driveway, the couch you're sitting on, the computer you're looking at or the house you're living in *has caused you to tithe irregularly or not give offerings when God directed you to do so ...* then you're eating at pagan shrines and worshipping pagan idols.

Anything that keeps you from giving into the Kingdom of God ... everything that keeps you from fulfilling his covenant is an idol.

If you're not tithing, then you're stealing from God according to Malachi 3:8 in the Message Bible which says:

"Begin by being honest. Do honest people rob

God? But you rob me day after day. You ask, 'How have we robbed you?' The tithe and the offering—that's how!"

If you've bought into the "fake it till you make it" lifestyle, if you're living from paycheck to Prozac but *yet can't help feed the hungry, clothe the naked or give to good ground ministries, then you're serving the wrong God.*

The scripture is clear. When you live according to the principles found in this *passage of scripture* in Ezekiel, then you will live *"... upright and well [and] shall live a full and true life."*

That's what God wants for you ... in fact, He wants you to see it.

That's why verse 5 of Ezekiel 18 in the Message Bible begins with the word imagine.

It's time for you to imagine yourself walking above and not beneath ... *as the head and not the tail*.

It's time for you to *imagine* all your bills are paid in full ... including your mortgage.

It's time for you to *imagine* your retirement accounts ... fully funded.

It's time for you to *imagine* ... you're walking in divine health.

It's time for you to *imagine* ... all your family members saved and filled with the Holy Ghost.

It's time for you to *imagine* you're operating in the end-time office of the giver ... and empowering ministries to reach the lost and disciple the found.

<u>It's time for you to *imagine* yourself ... the way God sees you</u>.

If you don't like where you are in life right now ... maybe it's time for you to realize you're not an ostrich with your head in the spiritual sand.

By the way, *for those who have their head in the sand ... do you realize what's exposed to Satan's boot?*

Make no mistake ... **God wants you to live a full, meaningful life ... but each of us is required to prove ourselves faithful and just** ... then we'll have the life that is really worth living.

Ephesians 2:10 in the Amplified Bible says:

> *"For we are God's [own] handiwork (His workmanship), recreated in Christ Jesus, [born anew] that we may do those good works which God predestined (planned beforehand) for us [taking paths which He prepared ahead of time], that we should walk in them [living the good life which He prearranged and made ready for us to live]."*

I strongly suggest that you put this scripture in your

smart phone, iPad, tablet or write this scripture down on an index card and carry it around with you ... until you have it memorized.

Personalizing the scripture makes it even more meaningful to you ... especially the last part of the verse which says, *"... living the good life which He prearranged and made ready for Harold and Bev to live."*

Now that's what I'm talking about.

The New Living Translation of Ephesians 2:10 says:

> *"For we are God's masterpiece. He has created us anew in Christ Jesus, so we can do the good things he planned for us long ago."*

Check out this personalization.

> ***"For Harold and Bev are God's masterpieces. He created them anew in Christ Jesus, so Harold and Bev can do the good things he planned for them long ago."***

The good life ... the good things *God has planned for you* ... doesn't include being so deeply in debt that you have to work 2 or 3 jobs just to make ends meet. The good life He planned for you doesn't include having the month run out before your money does.

God created you to be above and not beneath ... the head and not the tail ... so it's time that you and I to manifest His plans for our lives ... and it

begins ... by imagining ... *by seeing yourself the way God sees you ...* **as a Masterpiece.**

Day 10

How Free Are You?

Have you ever heard the expression ... "Do what I say, not what I do?"

I'm here to tell you that thought pattern may work *with certain members* of your family, or your friends and maybe even your co-workers ... but *it definitely does not carry God's Good Housekeeping Approval of Words well spoken.*

The statement, "Do what I say, not what I do," is at best hypocritical ... at worst, it's a *flimsy excuse for sin and/or personal foolishness.*

Your Heavenly Father wants you doing what He says ... PERIOD. PARAGRAPH.

Matthew 5:37 in the Amplified Bible says:

> *"Let your Yes be simply Yes, and your No be simply No; anything more than that comes from the evil one."*

The old saying, "**Say what you mean and mean what you say**," is a variation of a statement made by the Cheshire Cat in Lewis Carroll's *Alice In Wonder-*

land.

The Message Bible translation of Matthew 5:37 says:

> *"Just say 'yes' and 'no.' When you manipulate words to get your own way, you go wrong."*

Over the years, I've known and even worked with some people who will not lie to you ... but they don't tell you the whole truth.

If anyone doesn't tell the whole truth for whatever reason ... either to avoid embarrassment or reveal a weakness ... whatever the excuse or flawed logic ... they are manipulating words to get their own way.

And as the scripture says ... *that's where they go wrong.*

Perhaps the most definitive translation of Matthew 5:37 is found in the Contemporary English Version of the Bible:

> *"When you make a promise, say only 'Yes' or 'No.' Anything else comes from the devil."*

<u>The scripture is clear ... we are to say what we mean and mean what we say</u>.

Dr. Seuss once said:

> **"Be who you are and say what you feel, because those who mind don't matter and**

those who matter don't mind."

The best thing you can *feel, say or do ...* is found in the Word of God.

When you feel ... what He feels ... you can't go wrong.

When you say ... what He says ... you can't go wrong

When you do ... what He says do ... you can't go wrong.

We're to possess the words He speaks ... **we're to take ownership of His Holy Word**.

Years ago there was a movie called *Rush Hour* where an American detective was assigned to work with a *Chinese operative* who initially pretended to not speak English.

After several *moments of frustration*, the American detective annoyingly said, *"Do you understand the words that are coming out of my mouth?"*

Truthfully, *and in a manner of speaking*, that's what God is saying to each of us today.

Do we understand the words coming out of His mouth ... those He painstakingly put in His Holy Word?

And the question is *not just whether we're hearing His*

words, but are we obeying those words and following His directions?

Psalm 119:57 in the Amplified Bible says:

> *"You are my portion, O Lord; I have promised to keep Your words."*

If something is your portion ... *then according to the definitions I found in Strong's Concordance ...* you should take ownership of that portion.

Psalm 119:57 in the New Living Translation says:

> *"Lord, you are mine! I promise to obey your words!"*

We should fully understand His words and obey every single one of them.

The last part of Psalm 119:57 in the Message Bible says:

> *"... I promise to do everything you say."*

What God wants from us ... is total obedience to His Word.

Well, let me correct that statement.

What God wants from us ... is *immediate* total obedience to His Word.

Psalm 119:60 in the New Living Translation says:

> *"I will hurry, without delay, to obey your commands."*

Obeying God is not a matter of convenience or timing.

When God tells you to owe no man but to love Him … that's exactly what He means.

Romans 13:8 in the Amplified Bible says:

> *"Keep out of debt and owe no man anything, except to love one another; for he who loves his neighbor [who practices loving others] has fulfilled the Law [relating to one's fellowmen, meeting all its requirements]."*

The scripture doesn't say keep out of debt … *unless you have no other way to pay for your family trip to Disneyland.*

The scripture doesn't say keep out of debt … *unless you don't have the cash to buy your children all the toys they wanted for Christmas.*

The scripture doesn't say keep out of debt … *except when J.C. Penny's, Sakes Fifth Avenue, Wal-Mart or Macy's has all their clothing and accessories on sale.*

I could go on … but I think you're getting what it means to "keep out of debt."

Isn't it time we start obeying this command of God … **that we determine in our hearts to follow without hesitation or rationalization** … the Word of God when it comes to debt?

Proverbs 1:5 says:

> "A wise man will hear, and will increase learning; and a man of understanding shall attain unto wise counsels."

You may well need to re-program your financial mindset. For years, you've been seduced into the lifestyle of buy now, pay later *or more to the point, buy now and worry about it later.*

You can try to justify every step you take further into the bondage and the black hole of debt, *but when do you plan to get out* or at least stop digging the hole you're in?

W*h*en you're working to satisfy MasterCard's minimum payments and your money is not your own, *neither is it available to God's Kingdom, and* you're not free to obey His commands. In fact, <u>you have become a slave to the lenders</u>.

Proverbs 22:7 in the Contemporary English Version says:

> "The poor are ruled by the rich, and those who borrow are slaves of moneylenders."

In other words, *you're not free to serve* God because you haven't followed His commands.

I'm not seeking to put anyone into condemnation but the truth ... is the truth.

I want to ask you that question again, **"How free are you to serve God?"**

When you're working two jobs just to keep the collection agency from your door, you're not available to God.

The New Living Translation of 2 Timothy 2:4 says:

> *"Soldiers don't get tied up in the affairs of civilian life, for then they cannot please the officer who enlisted them."*

The King James Version says:

> *"No man that warreth entangleth himself with the affairs of this life; that he may please him who hath chosen him to be a soldier."*

The Hebrew word for borrow means:

"entangle, intertwine."

<u>*When we entangle ourselves with creditors to the point that we've lost our freedom to do what God called us to do*</u>, then we're not free and certainly not following His commands.

We have so much *stuff we need to take care of, pay for, insure, organize, fix, worry about, and keep track of ...* we've lost sight of what God saved us for. It wasn't just so we could go to heaven when we die ... it was to obey His commands and be about His business.

When it comes to obeying God's Word ... remember:

Financial tools and software will come and go ...

Investment brokers and counselors will win and lose ...

Corporate mergers will succeed and fail ...

Banks will be closed by regulators and new ones opened by investors ...

The economy will have recessions and depressions ...

But one thing will never change ... the Word of God ... the love of our Heavenly Father for His children ... and His forgiveness for our sins and stupidity.

When God tells us to do something ... He means it ... we'd best be doing what He's telling us to do.

Day 11

7, 8 or 9 Things You'll Like

Why do or should you give?

First, I give because I like to give.

I like giving because of the way it makes me feel.

If you've ever experienced the sparkle in a child's eye … or the tear in an adult's eye when you gave them a gift … whether *expected or unexpected* … then you know why I like giving.

If you've ever watched the expression of someone as they're informed their meal has already been paid for … *without them knowing you did it* … then you know why I like giving.

I also like giving … because it's God's nature to give … to bless.

James 1:17 in God's Word Translation says:

> "Every good present and every perfect gift comes from above, from the Father who made the sun, moon, and stars."

God loves giving good gifts … so … since I was created in "His image and after His likeness" (Gen 1:26) then I should like giving as well.

Second, and more importantly, God likes it when I give.

2 Corinthians 9:6-7 in the Message Bible says:

> "Remember: A stingy planter gets a stingy crop; a lavish planter gets a lavish crop. I want each of you to take plenty of time to think it over, and make up your own mind what you will give. That will protect you against sob stories and arm-twisting. <u>God loves it when the giver delights in the giving</u>."

Not only does God delight in your giving … it makes you indispensable to Him.

2 Corinthians 9:7 in the Amplified Bible says:

> "Let each one [give] as he has made up his own mind and purposed in his heart, not reluctantly or sorrowfully or under compulsion, for God loves (He takes pleasure in, prizes above other things, and is unwilling to abandon or to do without) a cheerful (joyous, "prompt to do it") giver [whose heart is in his giving]."

Third, I bless others by my giving.

Here are seven ways you bless others in your giving.

When you give a smile ... *you brighten up someone else's day.*

When you give your time ... *you bless someone with a need.*

When you listen to what someone has to say ... *you give value to their opinions and your friendship.*

When you greet someone with a handshake or a hug ... *you give them respect and recognition.*

When you give someone a helping hand ... *you become the hand of God on the earth.*

When you give loving kindness ... *you will receive more of what you've sown.*

When you give a gift ... *you're demonstrating the nature of your Heavenly Father.*

2 Corinthians 9:13 in God's WORD Translation says:

> *"You will honor God through this genuine act of service because of your commitment to spread the Good News of Christ and because of your generosity in sharing with them and everyone else."*

Fourth, I get blessed as others are blessed.

When you give ... whether to your church, a ministry or an individual ... you're blessed by your giving.

Ephesians 6:8 says:

> "Knowing that whatsoever good thing any man doeth, the same shall he receive of the Lord, whether he be bond or free."

What good thing I've done for others ... God is going to do for me. I gotta tell you ... I like the idea of God giving to me.

Galatians 6:7 in the Amplified Bible says:

> "Do not be deceived and deluded and misled; God will not allow Himself to be sneered at (scorned, disdained, or mocked by mere pretensions or professions, or by His precepts being set aside.) [He inevitably deludes himself who attempts to delude God.] For whatever a man sows, that and that only is what he will reap."

Deuteronomy 15:10 in the New Living Translation says:

> "Give generously to the poor, not grudgingly, for the Lord your <u>God will bless you in everything you do</u>."

It's impossible to give to others ... without you being blessed.

Deuteronomy 15:10 in the Message Bible says:

> "Give freely and spontaneously. Don't have a

stingy heart. The way you handle matters like this triggers God, your God's, blessing in everything you do, all your work and ventures. There are always going to be poor and needy people among you. So I command you: Always be generous, open purse and hands, give to your neighbors in trouble, your poor and hurting neighbors."

Fifth, I solve problems by my giving.

I remember someone years ago, when I worked with a mighty man of God who once received a smug, condescending letter from a Christian magazine editor/publisher/writer. (I list all three because I'm disguising the identity of this man who valued himself more highly than all others … combined.)

My mentor took the high road … whereas, I wanted to verbally take this egotistic writer out … but my mentor took the high road and wrote a very short conciliatory paragraph and sent the guy two Monte Blanc pens (valued at $300).

The man wrote back a gushing letter about the pens … with no mention of his presumed previous offense. In fact, the way he oohed and aahed over the gift … you'd never know he'd written such a vitriolic letter in the first place.

Proverbs 21:14 in the Message Bible says:

"A quietly given gift soothes an irritable person;

a heartfelt present cools a hot temper."

I want to say one more thing:

We worship God by our giving. There's a powerful sequence in Psalms 116 in the Amplified Bible. Let's start with verses 12-13.

> *"What will I give to the Lord [in return] for all His benefits toward me? [How can I repay Him for His precious blessings?] I will lift up the cup of salvation and call on the name of the Lord."*

Let's look at Psalm 116:14 in the New Living Translation.

> *"I will keep my promises to the Lord in the presence of all his people."*

Finally, Psalm 116:17.

> *"I will offer you a sacrifice of thanksgiving and call on the name of the Lord."*

By our giving, we please God ... and in turn ... we bless ourselves. We get satisfaction ... by blessing other people.

Philippians 4:18 in the King James Version tells us:

> *"But I have all, and abound: I am full, having re-*

ceived of Epaphroditus the things which were sent from you, an odour of a sweet smell, a sacrifice acceptable, wellpleasing to God."

Our giving needs to be well pleasing to God. When we are well pleasing to God ... <u>we are blessed in so many ways</u>.

There are some people who need this teaching. Get hold of it. Get it inside of you ... and let God *make a difference ... in your life*.

Charles Dickens said, **"No one is useless in this world who lightens the burden of others."**

Lighten the burden of others by being a giver. **Look for ways to bless others ... however you can ... and as often as you can.**

You will change their lives ... and you will change yours.

RichThoughts for Breakfast Volume 6

He Feels What You Feel

Day 12

*Jesus loves me this I know ...
for the Bible tells me so.
Little ones to him belong ... they
are weak but He is strong.
Yes, Jesus loves me
For the Bible tells me so.*

If you were raised in church, I'm sure you sang the words to that *popular* children's song.

Are those just words, or do you know how much <u>He really does love you</u>?

If you've ever heard the gospel message you know that God loved you enough to send Jesus to die for your sins. *Jesus also died so you could have good health and prosperity as well ... it's in the covenant.* **But He loves you even more than that.**

Hebrews 4:15 in the Amplified Bible says:

"For we do not have a High Priest Who is unable to understand and sympathize and have a shared feeling with our weaknesses and infirmities and liability to the assaults of temptation, but

One Who has been tempted in every respect as we are, yet without sinning."

Not only does Jesus love you … but *He understands, sympathizes and feels your weaknesses … your sicknesses … if you are suffering … and your responses to temptations.*

The Bible says Jesus is **touched by our humanity** … what we feel … He also experienced. That's why *He is the best role model that we could ever have to understand and help us.*

Consider the story of Mary, Martha and Lazarus.

Jesus was friends with this family. *It was Mary who anointed the Lord with perfume and wiped His feet with her hair (John 11:2)* and in verse 3, the sisters sent a message to Jesus saying, *"Lord, he whom You love [so well] is sick."*

Jesus not only knew Lazarus … **he was a close friend**.

No doubt Jesus had eaten in their home … spent time talking with them … because verse 5 says, *"… They were His dear friends, and He held them in loving esteem.]"*

Jesus sent word to the sisters that Lazarus' sickness *would not end in death* but *would bring glory to God*. I'm sure the sisters felt like God would be glorified by his "healing" because they had, no doubt, seen many healed at the Master's hand. *Jesus knew what was going to happen but they* **did not know the details**.

On the way to Bethany to see the family, *Jesus told his disciples that Lazarus was already dead (v. 14)*. When He finally arrived, Lazarus had been in the tomb for four days.

You know the story … Martha approached Jesus upon his arrival **and told him that Lazarus would be alive had he arrived sooner** (vs. 21, 22) *but that even now*, four days later, she demonstrated her faith by saying … **it wasn't too late for Jesus to act**.

Even though Jesus told Martha that Lazarus would rise again (v. 23) the scripture says that when He saw Mary *"… he groaned in the spirit, and was troubled"* (v. 33). In fact, verse 35 says, *"Jesus wept."*

Although Jesus knew He was about to raise Lazarus from the dead, *He still felt and expressed – the depths of human sorrow*.

You can take comfort in knowing that whatever you're going through, *Jesus has already experienced all pain … including loss, rejection, betrayal, and dying.* As our Savior and Redeemer, **He took all our sins to the cross and then forgave and continues to forgive us when we ask**.

He is touched by our humanity.

What affects us … affects him … *in our finances as*

<u>well as in other parts of our lives</u>.

I remember the first time I got the full revelation that if our giving moves us … *either joy or pain* … it moves God. He feels what we feel.

If you give your last dollar … **I mean the very last dollar you have in the world** … *He feels it … He feels your pain … He feels your faith.*

I remember once when my fine wife Bev and I had saved $25,000, *and that was a lot of money to us then* (and still is today).

God told us to use that $25,000 as a matching gift to help a young pastor challenge his congregation in *generating the down payment for their own church building and property.*

I had an uneasy peace about that significant gift. *I realize that "uneasy peace" is an interesting oxymoron.*

I was uneasy because that $25,000 had been designated for something I wanted. **<u>The opportunity was that God had it set aside for something else</u>**.

When I <u>mentally and spiritually</u> tapped into His plan for the money … **I got the peace**.

As far as I know, *no one in that particular congregation ever knew that we gave the gift or what it represented to us …* but God did *… and He's the only One who counts.* Truly, He felt what we initially felt … and our obedience to His direction brought His blessings.

Within a month, *our marketing company received a substantial increase in income.*

When the widow sowed her last two mites … Jesus sat right there and <u>felt her desperation and hope that somehow this would change her life</u> … **and it did**.

Mark 12:41-44 in the Message Bible says:

> *"Sitting across from the offering box, he was observing how the crowd tossed money in for the collection. Many of the rich were making large contributions. One poor widow came up and put in two small coins—a measly two cents. Jesus called his disciples over and said, "The truth is that this poor widow gave more to the collection than all the others put together. All the others gave what they'll never miss; she gave extravagantly what she couldn't afford—she gave her all."*

The precious seed sown by this widow woman moved Jesus … so much so that she was **memorialized in scripture** by the things He said about her.

You may be going through "stuff" … *but you've got to know that Jesus feels what you're feeling* … that's why it's important that you **give Him your faith to work with**. *You should always pray that what the enemy has meant for harm …* <u>God will turn to good</u>.

Genesis 50:20 says:

> *"But as for you, ye thought evil against me; but God meant it unto good, to bring to pass, as it is this day, to save much people alive."*

You should also never forget that the resurrection power of God being loosed in Lazarus' tomb was not the most significant thing that happened that day.

Luke 11:45 says:

> *"Then many of the Jews which came to Mary, and had seen the things which Jesus did, believed on him."*

You should always *ask that* **God be glorified** through your reaction to every adversity that life or the enemy throws your way.

When you respond by saying, "Why did this happen to me?" instead of, "My prayer is that the enemy gets no satisfaction from my response or anything negative that happens … and that You, God, be glorified in everything," **you fail to lift up the person of God in your trial or situation**.

In addition to looking for a way out of your current circumstance, situation and problem, *focus on how God can be glorified and the devil terrified by your response*.

In every situation of life … *you need to remember that*

He feels what you feel … **that He's touched by your humanity**. <u>You are not alone</u>.

As you travel down the trials and through the trials of life, *ask Him what you need to learn to better equip you to live a victorious life*. He designed you for victory.

2 Corinthians 1:4 in the Message Bible says:

> *"<u>He comes alongside us when we go through hard times</u>, and before you know it, he brings us alongside someone else who is going through hard times so that we can be there for that person just as God was there for us."*

What a powerful thought … **He comes alongside you when you're going through tough times**. *He feels what you feel … so we should do what He says … when He says do it.*

One more thing, He feels what you feel … so He can be right there by your side. *But He also expects us to be there for others as well.* In short, He wants us to **feel what others are feeling during their times of adversity**. He wants us to be there for them as well.

Now … that's something to think about.

Day 13

Are You in a Tight Spot?

Are you in a tight spot? Do you need an increase in salary or sales, more money, greater retirement benefits … perhaps it's a healing touch?

Bottom line … do you feel mounting pressures in any area has **placed you in a tight spot?**

King Saul found himself in a tight spot in 1 Samuel 13:5-14.

> *"The Philistines mustered a mighty army of 3,000 chariots, 6,000 charioteers, and as many warriors as the grains of sand on the seashore … The men of Israel saw what a tight spot they were in; and because they were hard pressed by the enemy, they tried to hide in caves, thickets, rocks, holes, and cisterns. Some of them crossed the Jordan River and escaped into the land of Gad and Gilead."*

You may think this Bible passage is of little consequence in your daily life … but nothing could be further from the truth. It is a classic example of tight spots we find ourselves in. Only the names, circumstances, and era we live in have changed.

In a sense, you face the Philistines every day.

Anything that takes your focus and attention off the things of God is an attack by a spiritual Philistine who's determined to take you captive or torture you.

The scripture offers a very clear directive on how to respond to an attack. It's found in 2 Corinthians 6:7. The Amplified Bible version says:

> "By [speaking] the word of truth, in the power of God, with the weapons of righteousness for the right hand [to attack] and for the left hand [to defend];"

If you don't respond to the attacks on your life with spiritual fortitude, you and those close to you, whether family, friend or co-worker, will seek ways of escape. Your reaction to adversity will either instill fear or faith ... peace or anxiety ... joy or sadness.

In the midst of an attack, believers can make unwise decisions because they're not seeking or depending upon the Lord ... their circumstances tend to overpower their knowledge of and obedience to God's Word. But God knows how to get you out of a tight spot.

King Saul watched his troops slip away in fear as he was waiting for the man of God to arrive (v. 8) so he decided to take things into his own hands. That's usually our biggest mistake.

Saul's Disobedience and Samuel's Rebuke

1 Samuel 13:9 in the New Living Translation says:

> *"So [Saul] demanded, 'Bring me the burnt offering and the peace offerings!' And Saul sacrificed the burnt offering himself."*

When Samuel arrived *he called Saul out* for being disobedient.

1 Samuel 13:11 in the New Living Translation says:

> *"… Samuel said, 'What is this you have done?'"*

Saul used the old sales technique … **deflect, defer and re-direct**.

Salesmen are taught that if they don't have a good answer for a prospective customer's question, they just deflect it. For instance, they say, "That's a good question."

Next, they defer the question by saying, "We'll get back to that in just a minute."

Then they re-direct the question to a conversational point which puts them back in charge of the sales call. "How you ever considered this …?"

Deflect, defer and re-direct is exactly what King Saul was trying to use on the prophet Samuel.

First, Saul deflected Samuel's question by saying, "It's not my fault." Saul pointed out that his men were scattering (v. 11).

Next, he deferred Samuel's question by pointing out that Samuel was late ... and since he didn't arrive when he said he would, the Philistines were ready to march against his troops.

Finally, he re-directed the conversation by saying that he didn't want to go to war before asking for the Lord's help so he *"... felt compelled to offer the burnt offering myself before you came."*

<u>May I suggest that you that you never try to deflect, defer and re-direct your mistakes to God</u>. If you make a mistake, fess up, repent, get up and move on. He knows it all anyway.

When you're in a tight spot ... **make a dedicated decision to guard against taking things into your own hands without God's direction**. It will keep you from making fatal mistakes.

That's exactly what happened to King Saul.

1 Samuel 13:13-14 in the Message Bible says:

> *"'How foolish!' Samuel exclaimed. 'You have not kept the command the LORD your God gave*

you. Had you kept it, the LORD would have established your kingdom over Israel forever. But now your kingdom must end, for the LORD has sought out a man after his own heart. The LORD has already appointed him to be the leader of his people, because you have not kept the LORD's command.'"

No matter how difficult or impossible the situations we face may appear ... we must always obey His instructions. When we take things into our own hands ... we mess up ... and that can cost your kingdom and ultimately your life.

The prophet went on to tell King Saul that God was going to find *"a man after his own heart."* One who would obey Him. **God's greatest desire is to be trusted.**

Simply said, a man or woman after God's own heart ... is one who always puts Him first even in the midst of a tight spot.

God gives us hope and direction on what to do when it seems that the attacks of natural and spiritual Philistines want to take us out.

Psalm 34:6 in the Amplified Bible says:

"This poor man cried, and the Lord heard him, and saved him out of all his troubles."

When you've got your back against the wall ... when it

seems the only mail box in your neighborhood filled up with bills and past due notices is yours … cry out to the Lord … and He will hear you … but more than that … He will save you from all your troubles, even the self-inflicted ones.

Not only that … He loves your effort … He puts the Angel of the Lord … around those *"… who fear Him [who revere and worship Him with awe] and each of them He delivers."* (Psalm 34:7)

If I'm in a tight spot … I'd rather have the angel of the Lord protecting me than the strongest person on the planet.

Psalm 34:8-9 says:

> *"O taste and see that the Lord [our God] is good! Blessed (happy, fortunate, to be envied) is the man who trusts and takes refuge in Him. O fear the Lord, you His saints [revere and worship Him]! For there is no want to those who truly revere and worship Him with godly fear."*

I suggest you read that last sentence again … when you're in a tight spot, isn't it comforting to know that *"… there is no want to those who truly revere and worship Him with godly fear."*

The scripture doesn't say there is "some want" … it says there is NO WANT for those who truly worship Him with godly fear.

Child of God, are you really getting a hold of this? There is NO, NONE, NADA WANT among those of us who truly worship the Lord with godly fear.

It gets even better ... verse 10 says *"... but they who seek (inquire of and require) the Lord [by right of their need and on the authority of His Word], none of them shall lack any beneficial thing."*

If you're in a tight spot ... you have the confidence, the knowledge and the scriptural assurance that *"... none ... shall lack any beneficial thing."*

Is having all your bills paid a beneficial thing ... is having a good job a beneficial thing ... is not having to worry about money a beneficial thing?

If you're in a tight spot ... feeling desperate and all alone ... don't run like Saul's men or feel forced into making foolish decisions like he did.

If you want to get out of a tight spot, follow the scriptural advice found in verses 6 and 7 in the Message Bible.

> *"When I was desperate, I called out, and GOD got me out of a tight spot. GOD's angel sets up a circle of protection around us while we pray."*

When you're in a tight spot ... remember the words of Psalm 34:9 in the Contemporary English Version which says:

> *"Honor the LORD! You are his special people.*

No one who honors the LORD will ever be in need."

And that's how you get out of a tight spot.

5 Things to Know Before You Invest

Day 14

With all the financial chicanery in the banking and investment arenas ... I've heard a growing number of believers question whether investing is wise or even scriptural.

Investing is scriptural *but it should not be entered into unadvisedly.* <u>I want to share with you five things you should consider before investing</u>.

1. **Educate Yourself.**

<u>Never invest in what you don't understand</u>. I could stop this teaching with just those seven words ... NEVER INVEST IN WHAT YOU DON'T UNDERSTAND.

Don't let anyone tell you that you can't understand. That's absurd.

Frankly, we have no business being involved with something we can't understand. And if someone can't explain the investment to you ... *you don't need to trust them ... especially if they say, "Just trust me."*

You may have a best friend ... a family member ... a next-door neighbor who understands or at least *says they understand* the ins and outs of investing ... *but that doesn't necessarily make it the truth.*

You may even have a friend who is a professional in the investing business but the bottom line is ... *the money you possess to invest is not theirs ... it's not even yours ...* it's God's.

<u>You're the one accountable for the stewardship of those funds ... not anybody else but you</u>. So I would strongly recommend that you take the time to *educate yourself on the fundamentals of investing.*

For instance, if you're advised to invest in mutual funds, *then you should understand the Morningstar rating system.* You should understand never to invest in anything that *doesn't have a rating of four or five stars.*

When it comes to buying stocks ... *you should decide whether you want to use a full-service stock broker* or make your own buy/sell decisions utilizing organizations like Scot Trade or E*TRADE.

Stop It. Someone just thought, "I'll never be able to learn this kind of information." *Yes, you can.* But you must first be determined to gain some very basic information.

After all, according to 1 Corinthians 2:16 *you have the mind of Christ and you hold His thoughts, feelings and purposes.*

I remember a dear lady named Emma from Memphis, Tennessee ... she was a high school graduate who went to trade school to become a dental hygienist. She was deeply in debt when she first joined the Debt Free Army. *Her husband was on disability and could not work* ... they had a mortgage, two vehicle payments and credit card debt.

As Emma was paying out of debt using our strategies ... *she began reading our material on the basics of investing*. Emma was determined to get out of debt and she was determined to gain a basic knowledge of investing and how it works.

Today, Emma enjoys the debt free life and looks forward each morning to reading the newspaper to see how her investments are doing. As Emma always says, "If I can do this ... anybody can."

2. A "Hot" Tip Will Get You Burned!

If the deal seems too good to be true ... *believe me* ... it is.

The get *rich quick* mentality is an *investment illusion* plus the scriptures continually warn against it.

When it comes to your investment mentality ... *I suggest you meditate on three verses from the richest man who ever lived*, **King Solomon**.

Proverbs 13:11 in the New Living Translation says:

> "Wealth from get-rich-quick schemes quickly disappears; wealth from hard work grows over time."

Proverbs 28:20 in the New Living Translation says:

> "The trustworthy person will get a rich reward, but a person who wants quick riches will get into trouble."

Proverbs 28:22 in the New Living Translation says:

> "Greedy people try to get rich quick but don't realize they're headed for poverty."

Check your heart. An impatient attitude will cause you to make unwise decisions.

3. Your Timing and Priorities.

It's important to honestly and accurately determine *whether or not* you're in the right place financially *to begin investing.*

Here's a revelation for you ... there will always be a great deal ... one too good to pass up.

Ecclesiastes 3:1 in the Message Bible says:

> "There's an opportune time to do things, a right time for everything on the earth."

Before investing, **I recommend you have all your high interest credit cards and consumer loans paid off**. These strategies alone will you a return of 12 to 24 percent depending on the interest rate.

It only makes sense that if you are investing money earning 12 percent and losing money at 18 percent on a credit card, you are in a losing position.

I also strongly recommend that you *have the equivalent of one month's income in your checking account* and a fund with three month's income in an interest-bearing account.

Some people call this strategy an "emergency or rainy-day fund." I personally don't like those terms *because if you save for an emergency or rainy day ... guess what you're going to get ... emergencies and rainy days*. I prefer to call it a "future fund."

I can tell you that it will be tempting to use the future fund as a "put and take" account ... but don't. It's unwise to put the money in a fund and then keep borrowing against it for things such as vacations, tuition, wedding expenses, etc.

My reason is simple ... what will you live on ... *if you're laid off ... if you're injured and unable to work?* The future fund does just that ... it will provide funds for your future. *If you need to save for tuition or weddings, include it in your plan.*

4. **Why Are You Investing – What's Your Strategy?**

<u>Before you begin to invest ... you need to have clearly defined financial goals</u>.

Are your investments for a college fund or retirement? If so, you're primarily interested in accumulating money for a future use. In this instance, you need investments that will grow over time such as real estate holdings, mutual funds or zero-coupon bonds.

If your goal is to create an income flow to live off of ... then I would recommend annuities, Treasury Bills and bonds. *Your number one priority is to make sure investments are safe ... so that you can live off the interest.*

Here is a simple rule of investing ... the greater the return, the higher the risk. <u>Every investor needs to determine their pain and anxiety threshold</u>.

At what point do you worry so much about your investments that you begin to lose sleep? That's your anxiety threshold.

As I was writing this teaching, Psalm 131:1 in the Contemporary English Version came to mind. It says:

> "I am not conceited, LORD, and I don't waste my time on impossible schemes."

The scripture gives some very definitive investment strategies.

Ecclesiastes 11:2 in the New Living Translation says:

> *"But divide your investments among many places, for you do not know what risks might lie ahead."*

Today's New International Version of Ecclesiastes 11:2 says:

> *"Invest in seven ventures, yes, in eight; you do not know what disaster may come upon the land."*

5. Remember whose money you're investing.

Pure and simple, we own nothing ... but we get to manage everything. We will be judged by our stewardship of what He entrusts to us.

It's His money ... so you want to make sure you're the wise servant. I suggest you re-read Matthew 25 on the parable of the talents.

Be mindful of Ecclesiastes 5:14 in the New Living Translation which says:

> *"Money is put into risky investments that turn sour, and everything is lost. In the end, there is nothing left to pass on to one's children."*

Finally, the best investment tip I can give you ... with the absolute highest rate of return ... is found in

Ecclesiastes 11:1 in the Message Bible which says:

> *"Be generous: Invest in acts of charity. Charity yields high returns."*

Don't forget to be kingdom-minded with your investments. God has the best investment guarantees.

7 Keys to Your Immediate Financial Release

Day 15

Do you work under oppressive conditions ... with unsympathetic employers ... *while living in a less than desirable neighborhood ... with barely enough food to feed your family* and little hope of ever breaking free of what's holding you back?

Welcome to Egypt.

It's important to understand that living in biblical Egypt as the children of Israel did *is paralleled to the existence that way too many believers face living in any town, USA or in many countries around the world.*

You can shout on this sensational morning ... yes, *rejoice in knowing that your financial deliverance is coming* just as surely as it came to the children of Israel in Egypt.

In order to experience an immediate financial release from the cruel financial taskmasters that you're dealing with ... there are seven keys you need to know.

First, you must recognize the ultimate source of

your deliverance.

You may have financial advisors ... *you may have read every book on getting out of debt* and *you may have created a spending plan.*

All of those things are good ... *but* the only way you will receive a true and lasting release from financial bondage *is when you put your eyes on the ultimate source of your deliverance.*

Second, you must recognize that you may have sold yourself into financial slavery.

How did you or anyone else get into debt? *You spoke yourself into debt.*

"Do you have a credit plan?"

"May I open a charge account?"

"Do I get a 10% discount the first time I use my new credit card?"

"What's the maximum amount of time you can finance my new car?"

"What's the smallest down payment I can make on our new home? Also, *can we have the closing costs rolled into the amount of the loan?"*

The list could go on ... but I think you're familiar on some level *with how so many believers have become financial road kill.*

Proverbs 6:2 in the New Living Translation says:

"If you have trapped yourself by your agreement and are caught by what you said."

Now here's the good news found in Proverbs 12:13 in the Amplified Bible which says:

"The wicked is [dangerously] snared by the transgression of his lips, but the [uncompromisingly] righteous shall come out of trouble."

You got yourself into debt by what you said … <u>you can also get yourself out of debt by what you say</u>.

Third, ask for forgiveness of your financial mistakes and sin.

If God were to ask you why you're in debt … what would you say?

Your answer might be "… because of my car payment or my second car payment or my house payment or my boat payment or my big screen flat panel LCD LED payment or my vacation payment or my time share payment or my new furniture payment or my credit card payments or, my department store payments" … are you beginning to see a pattern here?

The two prevalent words that are a part of the debt scenario described in the above paragraph are "my" and "payment."

What would you say if God were to ask you … did I tell you to buy that stuff or burden yourself with payments? Did you ask me what I thought before signing on the dotted line?

You got yourself into debt *but you're going to need His help to get out.*

Acts 26:18 in the Amplified Bible says:

> "To open their eyes that they may turn from darkness to light and from the power of Satan to God, so that they may thus receive forgiveness and release from their sins and a place and portion among those who are consecrated and purified by faith in Me."

If I were you … I'd ask Him now … if you haven't already … to forgive you of any and all transgressions … financial or otherwise.

Fourth, will your creditors assist in your release from financial bondage?

Psalm 144:11 in the Message Bible says:

> "Rescue me from the enemy sword, release me from the grip of those barbarians Who lie through their teeth, who shake your hand then knife you in the back."

You might wonder if it's fair to characterize your creditors as *barbarians*. Let's see.

Do credit card companies reveal up front the dangers of using their card *or do they lure you with seductive ads* and *the illusion of the lifestyles of the rich and famous* just by using their card?

Do your creditors tell you that if you skip those monthly payments during the holiday season that the *interest will continue to accumulate* and at an even faster rate?

Do the credit barbarians warn you up front about the consequences *if you can't make your monthly payments because you were laid off?*

Will the people who sold you that new car even with your bad credit allow you to *keep the car while you're looking for a new job?*

Credit barbarians are, at best, fair-weather friends and they're not going to lift a finger to facilitate your release from financial bondage … but God will. His mercies are renewed daily.

Fifth, the only way you'll ever be released from financial bondage is by asking the Ultimate Source for His assistance.

Jeremiah 29:12-14 in the Amplified Bible says:

> "Then you will call upon Me, and you will come

and pray to Me, and I will hear and heed you. Then you will seek Me, inquire for, and require Me [as a vital necessity] and find Me when you search for Me with all your heart. I will be found by you, says the Lord, and I will release you from captivity …"

When you call … He always answers … you're one of His favorites.

Psalm 86:7 in the Message Bible says:

"Every time I'm in trouble I call on you, confident that you'll answer."

Sixth, God will release you from captivity and give you more than you had before.

Jeremiah 30:3 in the Amplified Bible says:

"For, note well, the days are coming, says the Lord, when I will release from captivity My people Israel and Judah, says the Lord, and I will cause them to return to the land that I gave to their fathers, and they will possess it."

If you were blessed by this scripture … you're going to love Zechariah 9:11 in the Message Bible:

"And you, because of my blood covenant with you, I'll release your prisoners from their hopeless cells. Come home, hope-filled prisoners! This very day I'm declaring a double bonus—

everything you lost returned twice-over ... "

Hallelujah!!! This very day I'm declaring a double bonus. Are you ready for a double bonus?

Seventh, your immediate financial release from the bondage of debt is at hand.

Exodus 14:13 says:

> *"... Do not be afraid. Stand firm and you will see the deliverance the LORD will bring you today. The Egyptians you see today you will never see again."*

This is going to make you shout.

The Egyptians (your debtors) you see today ... *you will never see again.*

The mortgage Egyptian you see today ... *you will never see again.*

The credit card Egyptian you see today ... *you will never see again.*

The personal loan Egyptian you see today ... *you will never see again.*

Because your deliverance from financial suffering ... *is coming TODAY.*

Is there anything you have to do in the battle for your

financial freedom? Just follow the words of 2 Chronicles 20:17 which says:

> *"You will not have to fight this battle. Take up your positions; stand firm and see the deliverance the LORD will give you, Judah and Jerusalem. Do not be afraid; do not be discouraged. Go out to face them tomorrow, and the LORD will be with you."*

Not only is the Lord with you ... but He will never fail you.

Now it's time to stop acting like a slave and begin enjoying your financial freedom.

7 Ways to Show You Really Love the Lord

Day 16

Do you love the Lord?

If I were to ask most Christians if they love the Lord ... they would immediate say, *"Of course, I do. What kind of question is that?"*

Actually, *it's a very real and relevant question for every believer ... a question with important and far-reaching spiritual implications.*

John 14:23 in the Amplified Bible says:

> *"Jesus answered, If a person [really] loves Me, he will keep My word [obey My teaching]; and My Father will love him, and We will come to him and make Our home (abode, special dwelling place) with him."*

According to this scripture *the criteria for really loving the Lord* is to obey His teaching.

John 14:15 in the Amplified Bible says:

> *"If you [really] love Me, you will keep (obey) My*

commands."

What does God ask us to do in His Word? *Here are 7 ways to show your love for Him … by doing what He says:*

1. Confess our sins and ask for His forgiveness.

You can hide a lot of things … from a lot of people but **there is one thing you can never hide … your sins from God**. Even if you could hide your sins … *it would be an ignorant thing to do* … with immediate and eternal consequences.

Proverbs 28:13 in the Message Bible says:

> *"You can't whitewash your sins and get by with it; you find mercy by admitting and leaving them."*

Not only should we not whitewash our sins … we can't like them either.

1 John 1:10 in the Message Bible says:

> *"If we claim that we've never sinned, we out-and-out contradict God—make a liar out of him. A claim like that only shows off our ignorance of God."*

However, there's some great news when we obey His instruction.

1 John 1:9 in the Amplified Bible says:

> "If we [freely] admit that we have sinned and confess our sins, He is faithful and just (true to His own nature and promises) and will forgive our sins [dismiss our lawlessness] and [continuously] cleanse us from all unrighteousness [everything not in conformity to His will in purpose, thought, and action]."

2. Love one another as He first loved us.

Notice the progression in the next three scripture verses that I'm going to share with you next.

1 John 4:19 says:

> "We love him, because he first loved us."

The first scripture I learned as a boy was John 3:16:

> "For God so loved the world, that he gave his only begotten Son, that whosoever believeth in him should not perish, but have everlasting life."

John 13:34 says:

> "A new commandment I give unto you, That ye love one another; as I have loved you, that ye also love one another."

When our hearts are pure before the Lord … His grace will help us with this instruction.

3.   **Feed His sheep.**

God wants us feeding His sheep and *not just when things are convenient*. We can gain a powerful insight into the heart of God by reading Ezekiel 34:13-16 in the Amplified Bible:

> *"And I will bring them out from the peoples and gather them from the countries and will bring them to their own land; and I will feed them upon the mountains of Israel, by the watercourses, and in all the inhabited places of the country.*
>
> *"I will feed them with good pasture, and upon the high mountains of Israel shall their fold be; there shall they lie down in a good fold, and in a fat pasture shall they feed upon the mountains of Israel.*
>
> *"I will feed My sheep and I will cause them to lie down, says the Lord God.*
>
> *"I will seek that which was lost and bring back that which has strayed, and I will bandage the hurt and the crippled and will strengthen the weak and the sick, but I will destroy the fat and the strong [who have become hardhearted and perverse]; I will feed them with judgment and punishment."*

4.   **Care for the widows and the orphans.**

James 1:27 says:

> "External religious worship [religion as it is expressed in outward acts] that is pure and unblemished in the sight of God the Father is this: to visit and help and care for the orphans and widows in their affliction and need, and to keep oneself unspotted and uncontaminated from the world."

Pure religion is caring for the widows and orphans in their affliction and *not letting the world's view sway your belief system.* *Is this caring a part of your belief system?*

The way I read the scriptures ... helping the widows and the orphans is not optional. Rather it is the example of Christian love and compassion we show the world.

5.   Forgive those who have done us wrong.

Colossians 3:13 in the New International Version says:

> "Bear with each other and forgive whatever grievances you may have against one another. Forgive as the Lord forgave you."

The New Living Translation of Colossians 3:13 says:

> "Make allowance for each other's faults, and forgive anyone who offends you. Remember, the

Lord forgave you, so you must forgive others."

Ephesians 4:2 in the New Living Translation says:

"Always be humble and gentle. Be patient with each other, making allowance for each other's faults because of your love."

There is nowhere in the scripture where I have found the Word to say ignore the person … pass judgment on them … or condemn them. The Word simply says that we're to forgive one another even though it may not be easy.

<u>*To do any differently than what the Word says … means we have chosen to disobey*</u>.

Mark 11:26 in the Amplified Bible says:

"But if you do not forgive, neither will your Father in heaven forgive your failings and shortcomings."

6.   Obey the Ten Commandments.

It's important to remember that God gave us Ten Commandments … not Ten Suggestions … or Ten Recommendations.

Deuteronomy 8:1 says:

"All the commandments which I command thee this day shall ye observe to do …"

A little further in Deuteronomy 8 reveals some powerful promises and instructions in verses 11-13 in the Message Bible which says:

> *"Make sure you don't forget God, your God, by not keeping his commandments, his rules and regulations that I command you today. Make sure that when you eat and are satisfied, build pleasant houses and settle in, see your herds and flocks flourish and* **more and more money come in***, watch your standard of living going up and up."*

When we obey His Commandments we have the confidence in knowing that He will be delighting Himself over our obedience.

7. Be healthy, wealthy and wise.

Our Heavenly Father wants us to be healthy, wealthy and wise. 3 John 2 is the trifecta of His promises to us when it says:

> *"Beloved, I wish above all things that thou mayest prosper and be in health, even as thy soul prospereth."*

Notice the verse says *"... even as thy soul prospereth."* There is a direct correlation to your soul prospering. Your growth in the things of God is linked to your physical and financial prosperity.

The key to prosperity and success is spiritual

happiness and that only comes through a personal relationship with the Lord.

Proverbs 16:20 in the New Living Translation says:

> *"Those who listen to instruction will prosper; those who trust the Lord will be joyful."*

One final thought … when we've shown our love to the Lord by doing what He tells us to do … by obeying His instructions … by following His teachings … then we will receive a special visitation.

John 14:23 in the Amplified Bible says:

> *"Jesus answered, If a person [really] loves Me, he will keep My word [obey My teaching]; and My Father will love him, and We will come to him and make Our home (abode, special dwelling place) with him."*

Just think about that … He will come and make His home with you. Wow.

Success Secrets of Jesus

Day 17

I've taught on success a number of times before ... actually, I looked back ... I've taught on success on nine different days ... in the last six months.

> *"Success Is A Consequence"*
> *"7 Essential P ingredients For Success"*
> *"10 Commandments of Success"*
> *"Success or Just Getting By"*
> *"Why God Wants You to Be Successful"*
> *"10 Success Secrets of Joshua"*
> *"6 Steps to Success"*
> *"6 Differences Between Successful and Unsuccessful People"*
> *"6 More Differences Between Successful and Unsuccessful People"*

These powerful teachings have given the scriptural, practical and motivation keys to improving your performance and success in life.

It seems that almost every day someone is writing a new book about success ... that's great, as an author and an avid reader, I'm always happy when people write new books. Let me clarify that and say GOOD BOOKS ....

The Lord reminded me that ...

> If you want to be a lawyer ... **you study law**.
>
> If you want to be a doctor or a nurse ... **you study medicine**.
>
> If you want to be a cosmetologist ... **you study hair**.
>
> If you want to be a teacher ... **you study education**.
>
> If you want to be successful ... you study secrets of success ... *of the greatest man who ever lived* ... **Jesus, our Lord and Savior**.

I was reminded that Jesus was always improving Himself and that we shouldn't do any less.

Luke 2:52 ... And Jesus increased in wisdom and stature, and in favour with God and man.

I encourage you to read to this teaching with pen and paper in hand ... make notes and apply each of these strategies to your life.

Later, I encourage you to review and write down how they apply in your current situation and how God can use the truth of the revelation to take you to the next level.

Here are *The Success Strategies of Jesus of Nazareth*.

UNDERSTANDING YOUR PURPOSE

Success Strategy # 1: Jesus came to do the will of the Father.

John 6:38 says:

> "For I came down from heaven, not to do mine own will, but the will of him that sent me."

Success Strategy #2: Jesus knew who He was working for.

John 5:30 in the New Living Translation says:

> "But I do nothing without consulting the Father. I judge as I am told. And my judgment is absolutely just, because it is according to the will of God who sent me; it is not merely my own."

Success Strategy #3: Jesus was confident of His calling.

John 6:35 says:

> "And Jesus said unto them, I am the bread of life: he that cometh to me shall never hunger; and he that believeth on me shall never thirst."

Success Strategy #4: Jesus understood the necessity of goals.

Luke 2:49 says:

> "And He said unto them ... I must be about my Father's business."

Success Strategy #5: Jesus knew what happened to people without goals.

Matthew 15:14 says:

> " ... if the blind lead the blind, both shall fall into the ditch."

Success Strategy #6: Jesus was focused on His goals.

Luke 19:10 says:

> "For the Son of man is come to seek and save that which was lost."

Success Strategy #7: Jesus never lost sight of His goal.

John 17:4 says:

> "I have glorified thee on the earth: I have finished the work which thou gavest me to do."

Success Strategy #8: Jesus had goals that bene-

fited others.

John 10:10 in the New Living Translation says:

> "The thief's purpose is to steal and kill and destroy. My purpose is to give them a rich and satisfying life."

Success Strategy #9: Jesus took care of business.

Luke 2:49 says:

> "And he said unto them, How is it that ye sought me? wist ye not that I must be about my Father's business?"

Success Strategy #10: Jesus came to finish the work.

John 17:4 says:

> "I have glorified thee on the earth: I have finished the work which thou gavest me to do."

UNDERSTANDING YOUR POTENTIAL

Success Strategy #11: Jesus saw Himself with unlimited power.

Matthew 13:44-46 says:

> "… Jesus came and spake unto them, saying, All power is given unto me in heaven and in earth."

Success Strategy #12: Jesus taught excellence in everything He did.

Matthew 25:23 in the New Living Translation says:

> "The master said, 'Well done, my good and faithful servant. You have been faithful in handling this small amount, so now I will give you many more responsibilities. Let's celebrate together!'"

Success Strategy #13: Jesus knew the importance of speaking the right words.

Luke 6:45 says:

> "A good man out of the good treasure of his heart bringeth forth that which is good; and an evil man out of the evil treasure of his heart bringeth forth that which is evil: for of the abundance of the heart his mouth speaketh."

Success Strategy #14: Jesus understood that you needed to be a DOER instead of just a LISTENER.

Luke 6:49 in the New Living Translation says:

> "But anyone who listens and doesn't obey is like a person who builds a house without a foundation. When the floods sweep down against that house, it will crumble into a heap of ruins."

<u>MAXIMIZING YOUR STRENGTHS</u>

Success Strategy #15: Jesus was always improving Himself.

Luke 2:52 says:

> *"Jesus increased in wisdom and stature, and in favour with God and man."*

Success Strategy #16: Jesus guarded against time leaks.

John 9:4 in The Living Bible says:

> *"All of us must quickly carry out the task assigned us by the one who sent me for there is little time left before the night falls and all work comes to an end."*

Success Strategy #17: Jesus understood the importance of timing.

John 2:4 says:

> "Jesus saith unto her, Woman, what have I to do with thee? mine hour is not yet come."

Success Strategy #18: Jesus was aware of power leaks.

Mark 5:30 in the Amplified Bible says:

> *"And Jesus, recognizing in Himself that the power proceeding from Him had gone forth,*

turned around immediately in the crowd and said, Who touched My clothes?"

Success Strategy #19: Jesus guarded against information leaks.

Mark 4:11-12 in The Living Bible says:

> "He replied, 'You are permitted to know some truths about the Kingdom of God that are hidden to those outside the Kingdom: though they see and hear, they will not understand …'"

Success Strategy #20: Jesus approved of eliminating money leaks.

Luke 15:8 says:

> "… what woman having ten pieces of silver, if she lose one piece, doth not light a candle, and sweep the house, and seek diligently till she find it?"

Success Strategy #21: Jesus instructed those around Him to forget the past and move on.

John 8:11 says:

> "She said, No man, Lord. And Jesus said unto her, Neither do I condemn thee: go, and sin no more."

Success Strategy #22: Jesus was a good steward

of His God-given resources.

John 6:12-13 says:

> "When they were filled, he said unto his disciples, Gather up the fragments that remain, that nothing be lost. Therefore they gathered them together, and filled twelve baskets …"

Success Strategy #23: Jesus knew the value of praying when facing a big decision.

Matthew 26:42 says:

> "He went away again the second time, and prayed, saying, O my Father, if this cup may not pass away from me, except I drink it, thy will be done."

Success Strategy #24: Jesus believed in proper preparation.

Luke 9:51-52 says:

> "… it came to pass, when the time was come that he should be received up, he steadfastly set his face to go to Jerusalem, and sent messengers before his face: and they went, and entered into a village of the Samaritans, to make ready for him."

Success Strategy #25: Jesus began each day with the proper preparation.

Mark 1:35 says:

> *"And in the morning, rising up a great while before day, he went out, and departed into a solitary place, and there prayed."*

Success Strategy #26: Jesus instructed those around Him to forgive the past and move forward.

Luke 9:62 in the New Living Translation says:

> *"But Jesus told him, 'Anyone who puts a hand to the plow and then looks back is not fit for the Kingdom of God.'"*

Luke 9:62 in the Message Bible says:

> *"Jesus said, 'No procrastination. No backward looks. You can't put God's kingdom off till tomorrow. Seize the day.'"*

Day 18

The Successful Leadership Secrets of Jesus

Jesus is ... the greatest mentor, teacher and coach ever to draw a breath on planet earth ... and the best news of all ... He's also our personal Savior.

Here's what Jesus had to say about **DEVELOPING A LEADERSHIP TEAM**.

1.   **Jesus learned from others.** And for those of you in the network marketing business ... you can say He learned from His upline.

Luke 2:46 says:

> "And it came to pass, that after three days they found him in the temple, sitting in the midst of the doctors, both hearing them, and asking them questions."

2.   **Jesus expanded the vision of those He recruited.**

Mark 1:17 says:

> "… Jesus said unto them, Come ye after me, and I will make you to become fishers of men."

3. Jesus elevated the thinking processes of those He recruited.

Luke 9:54 says:

> "… when his disciples James and John saw this, they said, Lord, wilt thou that we command fire to come down from heaven, and consume them, even as Elias did? But he turned, and rebuked them, and said, Ye know not what manner of spirit ye are of. For the Son of man is not come to destroy men's lives, but to save them."

4. Jesus educated His staff.

Mark 9:31 says:

> "… he taught his disciples …"

5. Jesus taught His leadership team to be readers.

1 Timothy 4:13 says:

> "Till I come, give attendance to reading, to exhortation, to doctrine."

6. Jesus encouraged His staff to learn every-

thing they could about their jobs.

2 Timothy 2:15 says:

> *"Study to shew thyself approved unto God, a workman that needeth not to be ashamed, rightly dividing the word of truth."*

7. Jesus empowered others.

Matthew 10:1 says:

> *"… when he had called unto him his twelve disciples, he gave them power against unclean spirits, to cast them out and to heal all manner of sickness and all manner of disease."*

8. Jesus gave special attention to those He saw leadership ability in.

Mark 5:37 in the Amplified Bible says:

> *"And He permitted no one to accompany Him except Peter and James and John the brother of James."*

9. Jesus knew that every member of the team is important.

1 Corinthians 12:22 in the New Living Translation says:

> *"In fact, some of the parts that seem weakest*

and least important are really the most necessary."

10. Jesus stretched the members of His leadership team beyond what they thought personally possible.

Matthew 4:19 says:

"And he saith unto them, Follow me, and I will make you fishers of men."

WORKING WITH YOUR LEADERSHIP TEAM

11. Jesus taught that His team should always be ready to help others.

1 Timothy 6:18 says:

"That they do good, that they be rich in good works, ready to distribute, willing to communicate."

12. Jesus believed in delegation.

Luke 10:1 says:

"After these things the Lord appointed other seventy also, and sent them two and two before his face into every city and place, whither he himself would come."

13. Jesus gave His associates authority to act.

Matthew 28:18-20 says:

> *"And Jesus came and spake unto them, saying, All power is given unto me in heaven and in earth. Go ye therefore, and teach all nations, baptizing them in the name of the Father, and of the Son, and of the Holy Ghost: teaching them to observe all things whatsoever I have commanded you: and, lo, I am with you always ..."*

14. Jesus did not believe that failure automatically meant disqualification.

Matthew 26:34 says:

> *"Jesus said unto him [Simon Peter], Verily I say unto thee, that this night, before the cock crow, thou shalt deny me thrice."*

John 21:17 says:

> *"... Simon, son of Jonas, lovest thou me? ... thou knowest all things; thou knowest that I love thee. Jesus saith unto him, Feed my sheep."*

15. Jesus undergirded His associates with prayer.

Luke 22:31-32 says:

> *"And the Lord said, Simon, Simon, behold, Satan hath desired to have you, that he may sift you as wheat: but I have prayed for thee, that*

thy faith fail not: and when thou art converted, strengthen thy brethren."

**16.	Jesus believed that you should go the extra mile with your leadership team.**

Matthew 5:41 says:

"And whosoever shall compel thee to go a mile, go with him twain."

**17.	Jesus placed great emphasis on how His associates carried out their responsibility to others.**

Luke 16:12 says:

"… if ye have not been faithful in that which is another man's, who shall give you that which is your own?"

**18.	Jesus understood that a person with divided loyalties was unprofitable for service.**

Matthew 6:24 says:

"No man can serve two masters: for either he will hate the one, and love the other; or else he will hold to the one, and despise the other. Ye cannot serve God and mammon."

**19.	Jesus believed in loyalty among His associates.**

Mark 3:24-25 says:

> "… if a kingdom be divided against itself, that kingdom cannot stand. And if a house be divided against itself, that house cannot stand."

20. Jesus was moved by the efforts of other people.

Matthew 14:14 says:

> "And Jesus went forth, and saw a great multitude, and was moved with compassion toward them, and he healed their sick."

Jesus knew the wisdom of REWARDING His LEADERSHIP TEAM

21. Jesus knew His Boss rewarded service.

Matthew 25:20-21 in the Amplified Bible says:

> "… he who had received the five talents came and brought him five more, saying, Master, you entrusted to me five talents; see, here I gained five talents more. His master said unto him, Well done, you upright (honorable, admirable) and faithful servant! You have been faithful and trustworthy over a little; I will put you in charge of much …"

22. Jesus was reward-motivated.

Hebrews 12:2 says:

> "Looking unto Jesus … who for the joy that was set before him endured the cross …"

23. Jesus recognized members of His leadership team that did good work.

Ephesians 2:10 in the New Living Translation says:

> "For we are God's masterpiece. He has created us anew in Christ Jesus, so that we can do the good things he planned for us long ago."

24. Jesus believed in reward motivation for others.

Revelation 22:12 in the New Living Translation says:

> "See, I am coming soon, and my reward is with me, to repay all according to their deeds."

25. Jesus gave incentives to His leadership team.

John 14:2 says:

> "In my Father's house are many mansions: if it were not so, I would have told you. I go to prepare a place for you."

Day 19

The Greatest Mathematician I Ever Met

Let me ask you a question. Who was or is the great mathematician you've ever met?

— Your high school or college Algebra teacher?

— Maybe Albert Einstein before he died in 1955 at the age of 76?

By the way, Einstein didn't learn to tie his shoes until he was four years old … and a teacher once told Einstein's father:

"It doesn't matter what he does, he will never amount to anything."

Moving on …

— Perhaps it was some Nobel Prize winner who teaches at a university in or near your city?

But the ultimate … **the greatest Mathematician I**

ever met … is Jehovah Jireh, our Provider. He understands addition but *He's the greatest at multiplication*.

Genesis 1:28 says:

> *"And God blessed them, and God said unto them, Be fruitful, and multiply, and replenish the earth, and subdue it: and have dominion over the fish of the sea, and over the fowl of the air, and over every living thing that moveth upon the earth."*

The word multiply is the Hebrew word rabah (rah vah) (H7235) which according to Strong's Concordance means:

> **"be or become great; become many; become numerous; multiply (of people, animals, things); make great; and do much."**

The very first thing God told Adam wasn't to go to church … read his Bible … visit the sick … no, the very first thing He told him was *to multiply*.

The word rabah (rah vah) is translated 226 times in the King James Version of the Bible. It's *significant to note that 74 times it's translated as multiply … 40 times as increase …* 29 times as *much …* 24 times as *many …* and 8 times as *more*.

God used the word multiply with regards to animals … *populating the earth with man through Seth and Enos*.

However, it's clear to me that **God isn't just talking about population when He says multiply**.

In Genesis 17:2 God says:

> *"And I will make my covenant between me and thee, and will multiply thee exceedingly."*

You gotta also love Genesis 22:17 which says:

> *"That in blessing I will bless thee, and in multiplying I will multiply thy seed as the stars of the heaven, and as the sand which is upon the sea shore; and thy seed shall possess the gate of his enemies;"*

God wants to multiply everything … *your silver, gold, investments, real estate and all that you have.*

This is pretty clear in Deuteronomy 8:13 which says:

> *"And when thy herds and thy flocks multiply, and thy silver and thy gold is multiplied, and all that thou hast is multiplied;"*

The scripture says that **multiplication is involved in acquisition and possession of all that God has planned for you**.

Deuteronomy 8:1 says:

> *"All the commandments which I command thee*

this day shall ye observe to do, that ye may live, and multiply, and go in and possess the land which the LORD sware unto your fathers."

God also wants to promote you ... to multiply your success beyond that of family members who've gone before you.

Deuteronomy 30:5 says:

"And the LORD thy God will bring thee into the land which thy fathers possessed, and thou shalt possess it; and he will do thee good, and multiply thee above thy fathers."

God wants to multiply the length of your life through His wisdom ... which is His Word. Knowledge of His Word will *multiply the number of days that you have on planet earth.*

Proverbs 9:11 in the New Living Translation says:

"Wisdom will multiply your days and add years to your life."

When we live out His Word by obeying His commandments, then God will bless and *multiply you ... no matter where you live.*

There are some folks who believe God can only bless or multiply them in certain locations. The bottom line is *if you are where God wants you to be, He can bless you because you're following His divine directives.*

Deuteronomy 30:16 says:

> "In that I command thee this day to love the LORD thy God, to walk in his ways, and to keep his commandments and his statutes and his judgments, that thou mayest live and multiply: and the LORD thy God shall bless thee in the land whither thou goest to possess it."

The Greek word for multiply is plēthynō (ple floon no)(G4129) which means:

"to increase, to multiply."

Acts 9:31 gives us the secret to church growth.

> "Then had the churches rest throughout all Judaea and Galilee and Samaria, and were edified; and walking in the fear of the Lord, and in the comfort of the Holy Ghost, were multiplied."

The Message Bible translation of Acts 9:31 says:

> "Things calmed down after that and the church had smooth sailing for a while. All over the country—Judea, Samaria, Galilee—the church grew. They were permeated with a deep sense of reverence for God. **The Holy Spirit was with them, strengthening them. They prospered wonderfully.**"

As they were obedient to His principles and percepts ... multiplication took place through His Word.

Acts 9:24 says:

> "But the word of God grew and multiplied."

The Message Bible translation of Acts 9:24 says:

> "Meanwhile, the ministry of God's Word grew by leaps and bounds."

Have you been experiencing turbulence in your life ... *tossed to and fro by the storms*, **the adversities of everyday living?** Not only can you have peace in your daily life but your peace can be multiplied to you.

Delight on the words found in 2 Peter 1:2 which says:

> "Grace and peace be multiplied unto you through the knowledge of God, and of Jesus our Lord."

The Amplified Bible version of 2 Peter 1:4 says:

> "May grace (God's favor) and peace (which is perfect well-being, all necessary good, all spiritual prosperity, and freedom from fears and agitating passions and moral conflicts) be multiplied to you in [the full, personal, precise, and correct] knowledge of God and of Jesus our Lord."

Not only will God multiply wisdom, grace, favor and peace to you ... **He will give you seed to sow ... and then multiply it!**

2 Corinthians 9:10 in the Amplified Bible translation says:

> "And [God] Who provides seed for the sower and bread for eating will also provide and multiply your [resources for] sowing and increase the fruits of your righteousness [which manifests itself in active goodness, kindness, and charity]."

Hebrews 6:14 says:

> "Saying, Surely blessing I will bless thee, and multiplying I will multiply thee."

As I've mentioned several times in this teaching ... **God is serious about multiplying our blessings when we're obedient to His instructions**.

In Genesis 26, the people were experiencing an economic famine and hard times. People were fleeing the land and heading to Egypt ... but *God told Isaac to stay put. His obedience brought forth immediate manifestation.*

Genesis 26:12 says:

> "Then Isaac sowed in that land, and received in the same year an hundredfold: and the LORD blessed him."

That's what I call serious multiplication of a seed that is sown through obedience. You sow $1 and you get $100 in return.

I'm not making this up … consider the words of Mark 10:30 which says:

> *"But he shall receive an hundredfold now in this time, houses, and brethren, and sisters, and mothers, and children, and lands, with persecutions; and in the world to come eternal life."*

Now only does God want to bring multiplication into your life … **He wants you to experience manifestation now.**

<u>Genesis 26:12 says Isaac received the hundredfold return</u> *"in the same year."* **Mark 10:30 says that we can received the hundredfold return** *"now in this time."*

From the scripture it's very clear <u>the Greatest Mathematician you'll ever meet is ready to bring immediate multiplication into your life</u> … <u>but you've got to take the first step</u>.

Isn't this a good time?

God Is Not Weak (or Showdown at Mt. Carmel)

Day 20

One of my favorite Bible heroes is Elijah. I've always loved the story of Elijah and the 450 prophets of Baal. *I remember my mother reading it to me as a boy.*

I think the reason I liked the story so much was that the good guys won and the bad guys lost. As a child I could imagine it all in my mind's eye.

As you recall … King Ahab followed his wife Jezebel into evil. They led the people of Israel into worshipping Baal and Asherah. <u>Elijah, the prophet, showed up in town much to the King and Queen's regret and he challenged these prophets to a</u> … *Showdown at Mount Carmel* … where Elijah and the prophets of Baal were going to have a barbecue cook-off with some high stakes.

1 Kings 18:20-21 says:

> *"So Ahab summoned all the people of Israel and the prophets to Mount Carmel. Then Elijah stood*

in front of them and said, 'How much longer will you waver, hobbling between two opinions? If the Lord is God, follow him! But if Baal is God, then follow him!' But the people were completely silent."

Elijah even gave the prophets of Baal the choice of sacrificial bulls and let them go first.

1 Kings 18:22-24 in the New Living Translation says:

"Then Elijah said to them, "I am the only prophet of the Lord who is left, but Baal has 450 prophets. Now bring two bulls. The prophets of Baal may choose whichever one they wish and cut it into pieces and lay it on the wood of their altar, but without setting fire to it. I will prepare the other bull and lay it on the wood on the altar, but not set fire to it. Then call on the name of your god, and I will call on the name of the Lord. The god who answers by setting fire to the wood is the true God!" And all the people agreed."

Seems like a pretty straightforward challenge … you know, the kind you might find on the newest rendition of the TV show … "Survivors: Heroes and Villains."

The prophets of Baal did their best to get Baal to live up to his end of the bargain … but to no avail.

1 Kings 18:26 says:

"So they prepared one of the bulls and placed it

on the altar. Then they called on the name of Baal from morning until noontime, shouting, 'O Baal, answer us!' But there was no reply of any kind. Then they danced, hobbling around the altar they had made."

I really love this next part of the story.

1 Kings 18:27 in the Message Bible says:

"By noon, Elijah had started making fun of them, taunting, 'Call a little louder—he is a god, after all. Maybe he's off meditating somewhere or other, or maybe he's gotten involved in a project, or maybe he's on vacation. You don't suppose he's overslept, do you, and needs to be waked up?'"

In his comments … not only is Elijah having fun but he is also pointing out that *Baal wasn't a real god or else he didn't care about the prayers of his people*.

You know the rest of the story … the prophets of Baal failed … and God showed up … and showed off His mighty power … the prophets of Baal were slain by the sword … all 450 of them.

When the people needed a sign … a miracle … the direct intervention of God into their daily lives … He was not late … He was on time … and He definitely *wasn't weak*.

God manifested His power even though His

children had been foolish and drifted into idol worship. Without question, *He showed Himself strong on behalf of His power to be their God.* They were convinced.

In reading the scriptures, how many times did God deliver the children of Israel from adversity *before they questioned or rejected His assistance and direction once again?*

God will show Himself strong on your behalf ... if you will only trust in Him!

God is not a man that He should lie.

Numbers 23:19 says:

> *"God is not a man, that he should lie; neither the son of man, that he should repent: hath he said, and shall he not do it? or hath he spoken, and shall he not make it good?"*

God is not like man *that He is weak.* This powerful point is also found in Numbers 11.

The Israelites had grown weary of manna and complained to Moses to find them meat. Their complaint made God very angry with them.

Numbers 11:1 says:

> *"And when the people complained, it displeased the LORD: and the LORD heard it; and his*

anger was kindled; and the fire of the LORD burnt among them, and consumed them that were in the uttermost parts of the camp."

Although their attitude displeased the Lord, *He told Moses to tell them that the very next day* He would provide meat for them for a whole month!

Numbers 11:19-20 in the Message Bible says:

"And it won't be for just a day or two, or for five or ten or even twenty. You will eat it for a whole month until you gag and are sick of it. For you have rejected the Lord, who is here among you, and you have whined to him, saying, 'Why did we ever leave Egypt?'"

Now this miracle promise was so amazing that even Moses had a hard time believing it ... for He said to the Lord in Numbers 11:21:

"There are 600,000 men alone ... yet you promise them meat for a whole month! If we butcher all our flocks ... it won't be enough! We would have to catch every fish in the ocean to fulfill your promise!"

Verse 23 in the Living Bible gives us God's overpowering response to Moses' doubt:

"Then the Lord said to Moses, 'When did I become weak? ...'"

Precious Saint … <u>GOD is not in heaven **wringing** His hands over any situation you may be facing. He is not weak! He will show Himself mighty on your behalf.</u> *He just wants you to trust Him.*

If you're behind on your bills and your checking account is past empty … God is not weak.

If you're facing *foreclosure or eviction* … God is not weak.

If you *need a job or a better job* … God is not weak.

If your *children are being rebellious and your spouse is unfaithful* … remember … God is not weak.

Romans 4:20 in the Amplified Bible says:

> *"No unbelief or distrust made him waver (doubtingly question) concerning the promise of God, but he grew strong and was empowered by faith as he gave praise and glory to God."*

Not only is God not weak … He will show Himself strong on your behalf.

Psalm 68:28 in the New American Standard Version of the Bible says:

> *"Your God has commanded your strength; Show Yourself strong, O God, who have acted on our behalf."*

That's why you can walk in the same confidence as Elijah … knowing that God is on your side in every battle you face.

The odds against you don't matter.

The strength of the opposition is of no consequence.

The seeming impossibility of your deliverance does not move Him.

No matter how dire the circumstances … you will win because the great God Jehovah is on your side.

And His desire as expressed in Romans 8:31-32 is to bless and protect you.

> *"What then shall we say to these things? If God is for us, who can be against us? He who did not spare His own Son, but delivered Him up for us all, how shall He not with Him also freely give us all things?"*

Whatever situation, circumstance or problem you're facing today … **speak God's Word and know that He will always show Himself mighty on your behalf**.

God is not weak and He is not a man that He should lie … He is always right there with you … every moment of every day.

It's Not Behind You
It's in Front of You

Day 21

If you keep looking where you've been, then you'll never get where God wants you to go. **Your future is in front of you.**

It's time to quit looking in the rearview mirror ... and that's much more than a highway safety tip ... it's a spiritual truth ... that God wants us to get deep within our spirits.

Luke 9:62 in the New Century Version says:

> *"Jesus said, 'Anyone who begins to plow a field but keeps looking back is of no use in the kingdom of God.'"*

If you're waiting to bring in a new harvest ... *if you're wanting to reap the benefit of what you've sown* ... then *stop* looking back.

If someone has hurt you in the past ... *leave it there*. Don't harbor any resentment ... *don't add any painful memories to your mental play list.*

Unforgiveness is the one thing that will keep God from answering your prayers ... *simply because* ... He cannot answer what he does not hear.

Psalm 66:18 says:

> *"If I regard iniquity in my heart, the Lord will not hear me."*

Bottom line ... if you look back on the past to either *review, replay or re-live particular moments in time*, then the Word says you are of no use to the kingdom of God.

God's kingdom is heading in only one direction—forward. If you'll notice in Ephesians 6, God gives us no armor to put on our backs.

Don't recall sinful events for which you've been forgiven ... *if you look back and bring them into your remembrance ... then you've allowed the enemy to gain a foothold into your thought process.*

I've stated many times before that if God has forgiven you of your sins ... *He will not bring them up again.* He can't bring up ... what He doesn't remember.

Isaiah 43:25 in the Amplified Bible says:

> *"I, even I, am He Who blots out and cancels your transgressions, for My own sake, and <u>I will not remember your sins</u>."*

The Message Bible translation of Isaiah 43:25 says:

> "But I, yes I, am the one who takes care of your sins—that's what I do. <u>I don't keep a list of your sins</u>."

How can God bring up your past sins … *if He does remember them or even keep a list of them?*

God will not bring up your past … *but* the enemy will. But he can only get away with it if you let him. That's why you have to forget the past and move forward.

Philippians 3:13-15 in the New King James Version says:

> "… forgetting those things which are behind and reaching forward to those things which are ahead, I press toward the goal for the prize of the upward call of God in Christ Jesus."

The devil wants to make faces at you through the rear-view mirror of your life … but you must rebuke him … *claim your benefits as a born-again, demon-chasing Child of God.*

Psalm 103:1-2 says:

> "Bless the LORD, O my soul: and all that is within me, bless his holy name. Bless the LORD, O my soul, and forget not all his benefits."

Every believer should grab a hold of the phrase that

says, *"forget not all his benefits."*

The word benefit according to the Strong's Concordance is the Hebrew word gĕmuwl (gah moole) (H1576) which means:

"dealing, recompense, benefit."

In fact, the word benefit is found 19 times in 17 verses according to the Hebrew Concordance of the King James Bible. *Ten of those times the Hebrew word for benefit is translated as recompense.*

The word recompense is defined in dictionary.com with three "R's" ... they are:

"repay; remunerate; reward."

I'd say it's pretty important that you not forget your benefit package.

Now do you want to say it with me? "I've got benefits and I won't find them by looking in the rearview mirror of my life!"

Remember this ... **if you keeping looking where you've been, then you'll never get where He wants you to go**.

It's time to stop rehearsing our hurts ... *"forgetting those things which are behind."* If the things ... and that includes the people who have done us wrong ... are in the past ... then leave them there.

Quit thinking about what "might have been" and *take hold of what "can be"* as you allow God *to empower you during the next exciting phase of your life.*

Mark Twain once commented:

"I've been through some terrible things in my life including some that actually happened."

If you want to maximize your potential for the Kingdom, then you must learn how to manifest 2 Corinthians 2:5 in your life now!

"Casting down imaginations, and every high thing that exalteth itself against the knowledge of God, and bringing into captivity every though to the obedience of Christ."

Forget the past ... bring every thought into captivity ... NOW!

This is especially true when it comes to your finances. *If you've bought something you regret ... something you couldn't afford ... made an unwise investment,* then ask for forgiveness ... *deal with it and move on.*

It's time for us to stop talking about what has, could've or should've been ... God told us to occupy the land. *He did not encourage us to reminisce or commiserate about the past ...* He said, FORGET IT!

The only thing we should remember about the past is how God manifested His presence in our lives.

Child of God, you have benefits ... the scripture says that you will be recompensed by the Lord.

2 Samuel 22:25 says:

> *"Therefore the LORD hath recompensed me according to my righteousness; according to my cleanness in his eye sight."*

If you've obeyed His instructions ... *if you've stopped looking in the rear view mirror, then He will bless you ... remunerate you ... repay you ... reward you.*

Not only that, He will give you a fresh start.

2 Samuel 22:21-25 in the Message Bible says:

> *"God made my life complete when I placed all the pieces before him. When I cleaned up my act, he gave me a fresh start. Indeed, I've kept alert to God's ways; I haven't taken God for granted. Every day I review the ways he works, I try not to miss a trick. I feel put back together, and I'm watching my step. God rewrote the text of my life when I opened the book of my heart to his eyes."*

This message is so important that it's repeated again almost word for word in Psalm 18:20-24 in the Message Bible where it says:

> *"God made my life complete when I placed all the pieces before him. When I got my act to-*

gether, he gave me a fresh start. Now I'm alert to God's ways; I don't take God for granted. Every day I review the ways he works; I try not to miss a trick. I feel put back together, and I'm watching my step. God rewrote the text of my life when I opened the book of my heart to his eyes."

If you've been looking in the rearview mirror … ask God to forgive you … He's listening to you right now … if you're serious … <u>He's ready to hear and help you</u>.

Psalm 145:18 Message Bible says:

"God's there, listening for all who pray, for all who pray and mean it."

Stop looking at what's behind you … and drive straight ahead into your future … God's divine purpose and plan for your life.

You are a decision maker, a world changer, a destiny shaper, a mountain mover, and a wealth accumulator.

I believe God has great plans for you in the new year … but you will never see them by looking back.

God told us to "press" … to actively pursue … go after … to be focused and to stop at nothing … until we secure the prize … the high calling … that's what I call being a real winner for Him.

I want you to write this down. "My future is in front of me." In fact, personalize it … "<<Name>>'s future is in front of him."

One last exhortation … I heard Apostle Terra Nova from Brazil say several years ago, "I have seen my future and I've decided to live there."

Sounds like a pretty good idea to me.

Ask the Right Person the Right Questions

Day 22

If you knew that you had unlimited access to the greatest financial mind who ever lived, *would you tap into that reservoir of wisdom?*

This financial genius is smarter than Bill Gates ... shrewder than Warren Buffet ... more sophisticated than Donald Trump. Yet he's never been interviewed by Larry King or talked about by Jim Cramer.

However, I assure you ... *he has the greatest financial mind I've ever come in contact with.*

Are you ready to take advantage of this unique, free opportunity?

However, when it comes to giving financial advice ... *he does have one requirement* ... he wants his advice to be followed without hesitation *and regardless of the circumstances.*

Once he starts giving you advice ... he wants to know if you'll agree to ask his opinion before making any major financial decision. Without question, *he wants you making wise choices in every situation.*

Proverbs 2:9-11 in the New Living Translation says:

> *"Then you will understand what is right, just, and fair, and you will find the right way to go. For wisdom will enter your heart, and knowledge will fill you with joy. Wise choices will watch over you. Understanding will keep you safe."*

By now you've probably guessed that "he" is really "He."

So here's the question ... **if we want His help, then why are we not willing to ask for His advice in non-emergency situations**?

Several questions need to be asked ... as to why we don't ask for God's opinion before making any major purchase.

First, do we really care what He thinks?

Many a person ... yes, Christians ... think it's okay to buy something because ... it's on sale ... they can afford the payments ... but watch out. Even others will tell you it's a great deal ... you can't afford to pass up, but the real question is ... what does God think?

1 Samuel 14:36 in the New Living Translation says:

> *"Then Saul said, 'Let's chase the Philistines all*

night and plunder them until sunrise. Let's destroy every last one of them.' His men replied, 'We'll do whatever you think is best.' But the priest said, 'Let's ask God first.'"

King Saul got the approval of everybody *but the One who mattered the most*. As a consequence of his failure to ask God what He thought … *Saul's entire life, reign and legacy suffered the consequences.*

Second, do we understand how much He cares about our finances?

Too many believers either convince themselves or **listen to someone else's faulty reasoning** that God neither has the time or inclination to be concerned with the details of our personal financial situation.

Luke 12:7 in the Message Bible says:

> *"And he pays even greater attention to you, down to the last detail—even numbering the hairs on your head! So don't be intimidated by all this bully talk. You're worth more than a million canaries [sparrows]."*

If God has numbered the hairs on your head, doesn't it stand to reason that He'd be interested in the money in your checking account and the debt you owe? As the younger generation used to say to such nonsense: *"Duh!"*

Hebrews 4:15-16 in the Message Bible says:

> *"We don't have a priest who is out of touch with our reality. He's been through weakness and testing, experienced it all—all but the sin. So let's walk right up to him and get what he is so ready to give. Take the mercy, accept the help."*

<u>God is concerned about the realities of our lives and everything that we're facing</u>. We're that important to Him.

Third, we need to ask for His direction.

You can forget something on a grocery list … *you can forget to pick up the dry cleaning* … you can forget to do your homework … *you may even forget a loved one's birthday or your anniversary* … **but you should never EVER forget to ask God for His direction and help**.

<u>If we ask God for His help … He will help us … but if we don't … He won't</u>.

2 Chronicles 15:2 in the Message Bible says:

> *"God will stick with you as long as you stick with him. If you look for him he will let himself be found; but if you leave him he'll leave you."*

If we look for Him … we will find Him. Not only that … but He will stick with us until He's done everything He promised us.

Genesis 28:13 in the Message Bible says:

> "All the families of the Earth will bless themselves in you and your descendants. Yes. I'll stay with you, I'll protect you wherever you go, and I'll bring you back to this very ground. I'll stick with you until I've done everything I promised you."

There is one other good reason to ask God for His advice … and it's found in John 14:14 in the Amplified Bible which says:

> "Yes, ask me for anything in my name, and I will do it!"

Fourth, are we willing to accept the answer He gives us?

There is a school of thought that says it's easier to ask for forgiveness than permission.

If you think you're not going to get the answer you want despite the circumstances or evidence that it's a bad idea … *you may just choose to not ask for someone's opinion.*

If we want what we want when we want it, *then we don't want to ask for advice for fear it will not line up with what we want*. This is the way adults act like spoiled children.

We should ask for God's help and advice even though

we may not like the answer because we'll love the end result in days to come.

Proverbs 3:11-12 in The Living Bible says:

> *"Young man, do not resent it when God chastens and corrects you, for his punishment is proof of his love. Just as a father punishes a son he delights in to make him better, so the Lord corrects you."*

Fifth, you'll learn that delay does not mean denial.

When you ask for His advice … you will get His wisdom.

You will learn not to buy a house before you realize *whether or not you can make the mortgage payment* even with a job loss or change in your financial status.

You'll learn not to lease an expensive car with all the toys *before you discover whether or not you can easily afford the payments* … **or better** … **pay for it up front**.

You'll learn that time-sharing a condo is not a good investment long before you realize the maintenance fees have sky rocketed out of this world.

You'll learn about businesses that *should never have been started.*

You'll learn about financial pain and heartbreak that

could have been avoided.

You'll learn to never make a spending decision today based on money you think you will get tomorrow.

Sixth, we ask, and He'll answer.

When we ask ... even when we don't know what to do ... God will give us the answer.

Isaiah 48:17 in the Message Bible says:

> *"I am God, your God, who teaches you how to live right and well. I show you what to do, where to go."*

When you ask for His direction ... you'll never go wrong.

Proverbs 3:5-6 in the Message Bible says:

> *"Trust God from the bottom of your heart; don't try to figure out everything on your own. Listen for God's voice in everything you do, everywhere you go; he's the one who will keep you on track."*

It's foolish to make a financial or any other kind of decision without asking for His help.

Proverbs 18:13 in The Living Bible says:

> *"What a shame—Yes, how stupid to make a decision before knowing the facts."*

If you need financial advice and direction … go to the right source … the One who's never wrong and is always ready to help you out.

Jeremiah 33:3 in the New International Version gives us a plan.

> *"Call to me and I will answer you and tell you great and unsearchable things you do not know."*

Ask His opinion today … He's waiting for your call.

Day 23

Finding Peace in a Troubled World

If you listen to, watch or read the daily news it's filled to the *rim with grim. As believers we can choose to panic, worry or run in a corner and hide ... or realize our need and security is in Jesus Christ and His plan for us.*

When the angel of Jehovah appeared to Gideon ... *he was hiding in a winepress, threshing wheat in secret to protect it — and himself — from the Midianite invaders.* This was not a new way to thresh grain; *he was scared ... just trying to survive* and *not expecting anything in his situation to change.*

Look at how the angel of the Lord addresses Gideon. Judges 6:12 in the Amplified Bible says:

> *"And the Angel of the Lord appeared to him and said to him, The Lord is with you, you mighty man of [fearless] courage."*

I can imagine Gideon looking around to see if there was anybody else hiding on the floor.

I've noticed over the years that *when people are scared, they can jump right into a conversation without thinking.*

Notice Gideon's response in Judges 6:13 in the New Living Translation:

> *"'Sir,' Gideon replied, 'if the Lord is with us, why has all this happened to us? And where are all the miracles our ancestors told us about? Didn't they say, "The Lord brought us up out of Egypt"? But now the Lord has abandoned us and handed us over to the Midianites.'"*

At first Gideon *questioned this angel of the Lord and complained about everything that had been troubling his heart.*

How could God really love Israel? *How could God really care about Gideon when they were all in such distress, danger, and poverty?*

Gideon did not yet know whom he was speaking to. This angel spoke as Jehovah Himself and *when Gideon finally realized he'd been discussing politics and religion with God — face to face — he was rightfully terrified:*

Judges 6:14 in the Amplified Bible says:

> *"The Lord turned to him and said, Go in this your might, and you shall save Israel from the hand of Midian. Have I not sent you?"*

As I was reading verse 14 something stirred in my spirit that I want to share with you … *"Go in this your strength."*

The NLT says, *"Go in the strength you have and save Israel out of Midian's hand. Am I not sending you?"*

What he's saying is that you've got to take the first step … you've got to get out of the boat … *you have to make the initial effort … when you begin moving, a spiritual inertia takes place.*

It's like speaking in tongues, you've got to open your mouth and start talking.

Next let's look at Judges 6:22-24 which says:

> *"'Alas, O Lord GOD! For now I have seen the angel of the LORD face to face.' The LORD said to him, 'Peace to you, do not fear; you shall not die.' Then Gideon built an altar there to the LORD and named it The LORD is Peace."*

Where does God first reveal His name as The Lord is Peace – Jehovah-shalom? In the presence of a man who is desperately afraid … *a man who is worried and discouraged and has no peace in his heart.*

When Gideon's eyes were at last opened to see that **the Lord had taken a personal interest in his situation**, that God was present with him in the midst of his adversity and fear, he worshiped the Lord by a new name — *Jehovah-shalom*, The Lord is Peace.

In the days to come, the Lord was going to put Gideon in some less than peaceful situations. In some ways *Gideon would face more stresses and challenges than he had ever faced in his young life*. *Learning to be a "valiant warrior" wasn't going to be easy.*

But no matter what happened from this point on, *Gideon could look back to a moment in time when Jehovah-shalom said to him*, **"Peace to you, do not fear."**

If you feel as the enemy is attacking your finances *and trying to steal every dollar you have … just remember God is in the midst of your worry*. He is the God of peace. **True peace cannot be found in any other place than a right relationship with God.**

You cannot base your peace in the circumstances and situations of life. *You must not let your peace be centered in relationships, job or financial security or circumstance.*

This is your opportunity to discover that God is Jehovah-shalom.

As Paul wrote in Ephesians 2:14 in the Amplified Bible … *"He Himself is our peace."*

> *"For He is [Himself] our peace (our bond of unity and harmony). He has made us both [Jew and Gentile] one [body], and has broken down (destroyed, abolished) the hostile dividing wall between us."*

Once you really understand this and worship God as Jehovah-shalom, you can have peace no matter what storms blows in.

That's why Gideon didn't need 10,000 men … only 300 (Judges 7:7) … because God was His peace and power … *in the midst of seemingly overwhelming odds.*

Our Lord and Savior *also gives us a powerful promise just hours before He was crucified on the cross.* His disciples were in terrible turmoil, and things were about to get much worse. But in the midst of it all … Jesus has these words for us:

John 14:27 in the Amplified Translation says:

> *"Peace I leave with you; My [own] peace I now give and bequeath to you. Not as the world gives do I give to you. Do not let your hearts be troubled, neither let them be afraid. [Stop allowing yourselves to be agitated and disturbed; and do not permit yourselves to be fearful and intimidated and cowardly and unsettled.]"*

How many times in our daily lives do we allow ourselves to be agitated and our peace disturbed by the troubles around us?

The Lord's instructions are clear … *"Do not let your hearts be troubled."*

Now let's go further. Study the promises found in John

16:33 which says:

> *"I have told you these things, so that in Me you may have [perfect] peace and confidence. In the world you have tribulation and trials and distress and frustration; but be of good cheer [take courage; be confident, certain, undaunted]! For I have overcome the world. [I have deprived it of power to harm you and have conquered it for you.]"*

Not only are we told not to let our hearts be troubled … the scripture is telling us to *"be of good cheer [take courage; be confident, certain, undaunted]!"*

Be of good cheer … be happy even in the midst of your troubles, problems, situations and circumstances.

Here's a question for each of us.

When trouble rears its head and fear tries to move in and encamp in your heart and mind, where do you run to find peace?

Do your thoughts turn to another person to calm your spirit?

Are you tempted to find your peace in some fleshly desire?

Rather than accept some counterfeit brand of peace, go to Him whose promise will calm your soul. He, after all, is your Jehovah-shalom.

Psalm 34:6-10 in the New Living Translation has really been stirring in my spirit. It says:

> *"In my desperation I prayed, and the Lord listened; He saved me from all my troubles. For the angel of the Lord is a guard; he surrounds and defends all who fear him. Taste and see that the Lord is good. Oh, the joys of those who take refuge in him! Fear the Lord, you his godly people, for those who fear him will have all they need … and those who trust in the Lord will lack no good thing."*

If you're in a battle … *if you're seeking peace in a troubled world … you want to know that the One and Only person who can help you is listening.*

Psalm 86:6-7 in the Amplified Bible says:

> *"Give ear, O Lord, to my prayer; and listen to the cry of my supplications. In the day of my trouble I will call on You, for You will answer me."*

When you call on Him … He will always … **always answer you**.

Jeremiah 29:12-14 in the Amplified Bible says:

> *"Then you will call upon Me, and you will come and pray to Me, and I will hear and heed you. Then you will seek Me, inquire for, and require*

Me [as a vital necessity] and find Me when you search for Me with all your heart. I will be found by you, says the Lord, and I will release you from captivity ..."

Not only will God give you peace in the midst of a troubled world but He *"... will release you from captivity."*

No matter how you've been bound or hindered ... God is your peace and your deliverer.

Promises to Keep Before I Sleep

Day 24

Making promises is a godly thing!

God made the first promise. He promised that grass and trees would reproduce after their kind.

Genesis 1:11 says:

> "God said, 'Let the earth bring forth grass … and … trees … after their kind …"

God kept this promise.

Genesis 1:12 says:

> "And the earth brought forth grasses … and trees … after his kind."

God actually made 20,000 promises in His Word. The greater part are already fulfilled. Those that remain are being fulfilled.

The devil also makes promises. Notice how his first promise to mankind directly contradicts God's. God promises that if man ate of the tree of the forbidden fruit, he would die. *"… thou shalt surely die."* (Genesis 2:17)

Notice how Satan contradicts God with his own promise, *"… ye shall not surely die."* (Genesis 3:4)

When God asks why Adam and Eve disobeyed, Eve says she was deceived by a false promise.

Genesis 3:13 says:

> *"… The serpent beguiled (deceived) me and I did eat."*

Notice that it was Eve's dependence upon a false promise that brought about the devil's purpose in Eden. False promises and lies come from the devil.

John 8:44 in The Living Bible says:

> *"… You love to do the evil things he (the devil) does … for he is the father of liars!"*

Contrary to this, promises that can be depended on come from God's spirit.

John 14:16-17 in The Living Bible says: Working in us *"… He will never leave you. He is the Holy Spirit … who leads into all truth."*

Unfulfilled promises never bring about God's will. Instead they bring about Satan's will. Notice God's warning to those who make promises and don't keep them!!

Ecclesiastes 5:1-7 in The Living Bible says:

> "… Don't be a fool who doesn't even realize it is sinful to make rash promises to God...So when you talk to God and vow to him that you will do something, don't delay in doing it, for God has no pleasure in fools. Keep your promise to him. It is far better not to say you'll do something than to say you will and then not do it. In that case, your mouth is making you sin. Don't try to defend yourself by telling the messenger from God that it was all a mistake (to make the vow). That would make God very angry; and he might destroy your prosperity. Dreaming instead of doing is foolishness, and there is ruin in a flood of empty words …"

This stern warning comes to help us not to hurt us. For the Apostle Paul tells the Corinthians that keeping their promises to God will bring them overflowing abundance.

2 Corinthians 9:5-13 in The Living Bible says:

> "… I have asked these other brothers to arrive ahead of me to see that the gift you promised is on hand … remember this--if you give little, you will get little. A farmer who plants just a few seeds will get only a small crop, but if he plants much, he will reap much … Don't force anyone

to give more than he really wants to, for cheerful givers are the ones God prizes. God is able to make it (the amount you promised) up to you by giving you everything you need and more, so that there will not only be enough for your own needs, but plenty left over to give joyfully to others. It is as the Scriptures say: 'The godly man gives generously to the poor. His good deeds will be an honor to him forever.' For God, who gives seed to the farmer to plant, and later on, good crops to harvest and eat, will give you more and more seed to plant and will make it grow so that you can give away more and more fruit from your harvest. Yes, God will give you much so that you can give away much ... Those you help will be glad ... for this proof that your deeds are as good as your doctrine."

There is another verse of warning to those who would leave a promise made unfulfilled.

Deuteronomy 23:21 in the Amplified Bible says:

"When you make a vow to the Lord your God, you shall not be slack in paying it, for the Lord your God will surely require it of you, and slackness would be sin in you."

Notice that an unfulfilled promise becomes sin "in" the person who fails to pay it.

Note that fulfilling promises is very valuable to the believer ... for those who do can confidently call upon

God for help when trouble comes.

Deuteronomy 23:21 in the Amplified Bible says:

> "Offer unto God thanksgiving; and pay thy vows unto the most High: and call upon me in the day of trouble: I will deliver thee ..."

As I mentioned in the beginning of the teaching there are over 20,000 promises God made to us. Thus far, we've talked how we're to keep our promises to Him.

Now I want to share seven financial promises that God has made to us.

First, God promised that seedtime and harvest are perpetual ... eternal.

Genesis 8:22 says:

> "While the earth remaineth, seedtime and harvest, and cold and heat, and summer and winter, and day and night shall not cease."

As long as the earth remains ... that means **seedtime (sowing, giving) and harvest (reaping, receiving) will be here till the end of time**.

Second, God promises that He will supply every need we have.

Philippians 4:19 in the Amplified Bible says:

> *"And my God will liberally supply (fill to the full) your every need according to His riches in glory in Christ Jesus."*

Fill to the full … doesn't mean barely getting by … or provisions just for basic survival.

Not living under the stress of debt and lack is definitely a need in our lives.

Third, He promised if we sow … that we would reap.

Galatians 6:7 in the Amplified Bible says:

> *"Do not be deceived and deluded and misled; God will not allow Himself to be sneered at (scorned, disdained, or mocked by mere pretensions or professions, or by His precepts being set aside.) [He inevitably deludes himself who attempts to delude God.] For whatever a man sows, that and that only is what he will reap."*

The scripture says what "we sow" that "we shall reap." It's not what somebody else sows … it's what we sow.

Fourth, God promised seed to the sower.

Second Corinthians 9:10 AMP says:

> "And [God] Who provides seed for the sower and bread for eating will also provide and multiply your [resources for] sowing and increase the fruits of your righteousness [which manifests itself in active goodness, kindness, and charity]."

The key phrase in this verse is that God will provide "… seed for the sower." **If you're not a sower, then He's not providing.**

Fifth, God promised if we're diligent in the workplace we will lack for nothing.

1 Thessalonians 4:11-12 in the King James Version of the Bible:

> "And that ye study to be quiet, and to do your own business, and to work with your own hands, as we commanded you; That ye may walk honestly toward them that are without, and that <u>ye may have lack of nothing</u>."

1 Thessalonians 4:12 which in The Living Bible says:

> "As a result, people who are not Christians will trust and respect you, and you will not need to depend on others for enough money to pay your bills."

Sixth, God promised the kind of return we will receive when we sow as He directs.

Matthew 13:23 says:

> "But he that received seed into the good ground is he that heareth the word, and understandeth it; which also beareth fruit, and bringeth forth, some an hundredfold, some sixty, some thirty."

Seventh, God promised that if you obey His instructions ... you will be rich.

Isaiah 1:19 in The Living Bible which says:

> "If you will only let me help you, if you will only obey, then I will make you rich!"

God wants to be your financial planner ... He will make you very rich.

The key point of this teaching is how to become rich ... so it's important to fully understand that when the scripture says, *"If you will only let me help you, if you will only obey ..."* it clearly means we have a choice.

One final scripture.

Hebrews 10:23 in the Amplified Bible says:

> "So let us seize and hold fast and retain without wavering the hope we cherish and confess and our acknowledgement of it, for He Who promised is reliable (sure) and faithful to His word."

God wants to ... change ... your life ... today!

You Don't Need to Know It All

Day 25

Have you ever met someone who felt they had all the answers to life's challenges and opportunities?

It's fairly clear that without exception ... *anyone who thinks that he/she knows it all ... doesn't.*

If you need to make an important decision ... *if you need financial guidance ... or spiritual wisdom*, then I encourage you to follow the *scriptural* insight found in Proverbs 15:22 in the Amplified Bible:

> "Where there is no counsel, purposes are frustrated, but with many counselors they are accomplished."

The New Living Translation of Proverbs 15:22 says:

> "Plans go wrong for lack of advice; many advisers bring success."

If you want to succeed in life ... it's best to seek out advisers or counselors who can guide you in the area of investments, debt elimination, real estate, networking, business plans, estate planning and much more.

I believe in getting all the advice I can prior to making a decision. *Such an approach is not only wise ... it's scriptural.*

We find many scriptures that warn us about the disadvantages and pitfalls of not having good counselors and advisers.

Proverbs 11:14 in the Amplified Bible says:

"Where no wise guidance is, the people fall, but in the multitude of counselors there is safety."

Proverbs 24:6 in the Amplified Bible says:

"For by wise counsel you can wage your war, and in an abundance of counselors there is victory and safety."

Proverbs 24:6 in the New Living Translation says:

"So don't go to war without wise guidance; victory depends on having many advisers."

Your victory ... your success is in part dependent on your ability to have good counselors and advisers speaking into your life.

The Message Bible translation of 15:22 says:

"Refuse good advice and watch your plans fail;

take good counsel and watch them succeed."

Never get estate planning and/or investment advice from one person. *Some sales people have multiple agendas … yes, they want to help you … but they also want to help themselves with a nice commission check based on what program you buy from them.*

Don't get me wrong … there is nothing unethical about a sales person earning a commission … but on occasion their vested interest supersedes yours.

For instance, some life insurance representatives may try to sell you a whole life insurance policy instead of term insurance because the whole life plan carries a higher commission.

Some professionals have tunnel vision … for instance, *I've had CPAs advise me against paying off my house because of the home interest deduction.*

A credit counselor with a secular attitude and even some "Christian" credit agencies will have trouble with you tithing *because they feel you need all your resources to pay off your debts.* **They just don't understand the spiritual consequences of what they're asking you to do because they don't believe that the Word works.**

I'm not saying that you shouldn't have a financial advisor … I have two of them. I like having different perspectives when it comes of my effective stewardship of what God has entrusted to me.

Always! ALWAYS! Measure any financial advice that you're given against the Word of God. If the advice doesn't line up with the Word, then don't do it … regardless of how much "sense" it seems to make. PERIOD. PARAGRAPH.

As I travel the nations I'm frequently asked by people if I'll be their mentor. That is, it's a question often asked, *answered*, but seldom followed up on.

I remember the time one ambitious young man asked me if I'd be his personal mentor. I asked, "Why me?" He said, "You talk more about debt free living and rich thoughts than anyone I know of."

I asked him if I could assemble a team of 100 of the best success coaches and personal mentors, would he be interested. He said, "Absolutely!"

Then he asked, "Is it a seminar? An online program? How does it work? How long would I have access to them?"

I asked, "Would you be interested in immediate and unlimited access to these great writers, teachers and speakers?" Once again, his eyes sparkled as he said, "Are you kidding?"

Then I told him that getting these 100 inspirational leaders together in one place might be difficult … so would it be acceptable if we took accounts of the lives, teachings and rich thoughts of these folks … recorded the best of all their collected wisdom into one volume

… then asked if he would be interested in purchasing such a priceless collection?

He told me that he had been to one of those weekend seminars where one dude charged him $2,500 just to hear him talk and pitch his $5,000 wealth accumulation system.

Then he said, "100 of the best and most successful teachers and mentors offering their best stuff. Just tell me how much … if it's too expensive, I may need to put it on my credit card."

I said, "Relax, I'm sure you call afford this priceless book," as I reached into my briefcase and pulled out my Bible.

His face probably looked the same way you felt in hearing these words … disappointed. But get real … think about it.

The Bible is without question the greatest success guide for debt-free living ever written.

Within its 66 books you will find success and failure, tragedy and triumph, betrayal and forgiveness, despair and hope, hurt and healing, doubt and faith, decisions made and consequences experienced … the promise of eternal life then and abundant life now.

2 Timothy 3:16-17 in the Amplified Bible says:

> "*Every Scripture is God-breathed, (given by His*

inspiration) and profitable for instruction, for reproof and conviction of sin, for correction of error and discipline in obedience, [and] for training in righteousness (in holy living, in conformity to God's will in thought, purpose, and action), so that the man of God may be complete and proficient, well fitted and thoroughly equipped for every good work."

The Psalmist had it right in the Amplified Bible translation of Psalm 119:99 which says:

"I have better understanding and deeper insight than all my teachers [because of Your word], for Your testimonies are my meditation."

Child of God, here's my challenge for you … **set aside a specific time each day to spend time with the greatest mentor of all … the Holy Spirit**. Ask Him to reveal the financial revelations you need to know right now.

Isaiah 54:11 in the Message Bible says:

"… All your children will have God for their teacher— what a mentor for your children! You'll be built solid, grounded in righteousness, far from any trouble—nothing to fear! far from terror—it won't even come close … This is what God's servants can expect. I'LL SEE TO IT THAT EVERYTHING WORKS OUT FOR THE BEST. God's Decree."

Even when you have great advisers, counselors and mentors … there is going to come a point … where you will need to weigh all the suggestions and recommendations based on what the Word of God says … and just do it.

Ultimately, **you'll be the one on Judgment Day who must give an account for the effectiveness of your stewardship**.

For nearly twenty years I worked with Brother John Avanzini, my dear friend and mentor. Brother John looked to me for creative insight and practical suggestions as to how we could more effectively get the body of Christ out of debt and into His abundance.

When presenting him with my ideas … I would frequently tell him that I was of no value to him if I didn't speak plainly and share my suggestions. However, I would remind him and myself whose name was on the front of the building. *It was his, not mine.* It was Brother John who made the final determination on every submitted idea. But with Brother John, *I was confident that God would be glorified and the devil terrified by the decisions he made.*

2 Samuel 15:15 in the New Living Translation sums it up.

> "'We are with you,' his advisers replied. 'Do what you think is best.'"

You don't have to be a know it all because you

have a personal relationship with Someone who does know it all.

Trust Him.

Day 26

Nobody Could Ever Love Somebody Like Me

I'm going to share a statement that I've heard way too often … from believers around the world.

Nobody could ever love somebody like me.

Devil, here you go lying again.

First, God loves you and truthfully, that's something that will never change. There is a scripture which proves God's love beyond a shadow of a doubt.

John 3:16 says:

> "For God so loved the world that he gave his only begotten Son, that whosoever believeth in him should not perish, but have everlasting life."

According to Strong's Concordance, the Greek word for whosoever is pas (G3956) and it means:

> "each, every, any, all, the whole, everyone, all things, everything."

As we learned earlier ... ALL MEANS EVERYTHING.

Second, we're to love other people as He first loved us.

Mark 12:31 says:

> "And the second is like, namely this, Thou shalt love thy neighbour as thyself. There is none other commandment greater than these."

John 13:34 tells us:

> "A new commandment I give unto you, That ye love one another; as I have loved you, that ye also love one another."

God loves you *whether you have bad breath or not.*

God loves you whether you're rich or poor.

God loves you whether you're *skinny or fat, ugly or beautiful, a college graduate or a grammar school drop-out.*

God loves you whether you're a Republican or a Democrat ... a liberal or a conservative ... though I do have a personal opinion on who He loves best. (Just kidding.)

God loves you whether you're *single, divorced, married or remarried three times.*

God loves you even when you mess up … as long as you get up, repent and move on.

Not only does God love you … but He expects you to love others just as He loves you.

God does not pick and choose whom He loves … by any criteria or list of faults that He is overlooking.

God loves everybody … and He expects the same of us.

Romans 13:8 says:

> *"Owe no man anything, but to love one another: for he that loveth another hath fulfilled the law."*

1 John 5:1-3 in the Amplified Bible says:

> *"EVERYONE WHO believes (adheres to, trusts, and relies on the fact) that Jesus is the Christ (the Messiah) is a born-again child of God; and everyone who loves the Father also loves the one born of Him (His offspring). By this we come to know (recognize and understand) that we love the children of God: when we love God and obey His commands (orders, charges)--[when we keep His ordinances and are mindful of His precepts and His teaching]. For the [true] love of God is this: that we do His commands [keep His ordinances and are mindful of His precepts and teaching]. And these orders of His are not irksome (burdensome, oppressive, or grievous)."*

Bottom line … if want to love and please God, then you will obey His precepts and teachings.

When people doubt God's love, it is *generally based on something negative that has happened to them* or *some blessings they feel others received and they have not.*

One thing you need to know. **God loves everyone … regardless!** However, *He does reward people based on their faith in His principles*. If someone else knows *how to put God's principles to work more than you … they will undoubtedly reap more benefits than you …* but you can change that when you better understand the Word.

Third, God loves you even when nobody else is around you.

John 16:27 in the New Century Version says:

> *"The Father himself loves you. He loves you because you loved me and believed that I came from God."*

God loves you … no matter where you are … because you love Him and gave your life to Him. It's just that simple.

Psalm 59:10 in the New Century Version says:

> *"My God loves me, and he goes in front of me. He will help me defeat my enemies."*

Fourth, when God loves you and you love others … He will never leave you.

Deuteronomy 31:6 in the New Living Translation says:

> "So be strong and courageous! Do not be afraid and do not panic before them. For the Lord your God will personally go ahead of you. He will neither fail you nor abandon you."

Hebrews 13:5 in the Amplified Bible says:

> "Let your character or moral disposition be free from love of money [including greed, avarice, lust, and craving for earthly possessions] and be satisfied with your present [circumstances and with what you have]; for He [God] Himself has said, I will not in any way fail you nor give you up nor leave you without support. [I will] not, [I will] not, [I will] not in any degree leave you helpless nor forsake nor let [you] down (relax My hold on you)! [Assuredly not!]"

Not only are you never alone … but God will always protect those He loves and who loves Him.

Psalm 59:17 in the New Century Version says:

> "God, my strength, I will sing praises to you. God, my defender, you are the God who loves me."

Isn't it fun exposing lies perpetrated by the devil?

Fifth, when you put God first, then you will experience the God kind of love from others.

I want to share with you two testimonies that bear witness to this fifth point.

A good friend, a single attorney and Superior Court Judge, who had never been married was looking for a wife. He was 39 and dating every girl he met regardless of where he met them … although he did bring them to church with him.

Most of these girls *were as lost as a goose in a blizzard* and the Judge was a Christian.

I remember praying with him one Sunday night outside our church in North Carolina. I told him when he put God first in his life that the right woman, the marrying kind, would manifest in his life. He committed to put God first.

In less than a month, a godly young woman ten years younger than him entered his life … they later married and had six wonderful children.

In addition, when my oldest son was a sophomore in college he said he wanted to meet someone he could marry, and although he didn't drink or do drugs, he would go to clubs to meet girls.

I remember a conversation with him in the back of my father's store. I told him that he would never find the kind of girl he wanted to marry in a club. I told him the girls who went clubbing were looking for something that didn't exist in their lives.

He frankly told me that the kind of girl I wanted for him didn't exist ... an attractive Christian virgin. He said that 9 out of 10 of the girls that he knew weren't virgins and the Christian girls weren't attractive.

I explained to him ... as I did to my Superior Court Judge friend ... that if he put God first in his life ... *the attractive Christian virgin would manifest in his life*. He agreed and we prayed right there in Dad's Western Auto store. I can see the image in my mind as if it were yesterday.

Within two weeks "the one" walked into his life ... a very beautiful young lady with strict Christian morals. *They later married and now have two of the smartest, cutest and most precious grandchildren to ever draw a breath.*

Put God first ... then He will bring the right person into your life ... someone to love you the way God says love should be.

Day 27

7 Reasons to Do What Is Good

This morning as I read Amos 5:14-15 in the Message Bible ... my spirit was stirred.

> "*Do what is good* and run from evil so that you may live! Then the Lord God of Heaven's Armies will be your helper, just as you have claimed. Hate evil and love what is good; turn your courts into true halls of justice. Perhaps even yet the Lord God of Heaven's Armies will have mercy on the remnant of his people."

The first four words of this passage detail how we should act and react in our daily Christian living. Here are seven reasons why we should "Do What Is Good."

1. Doing What Is Good is personally taught by God.

My parents taught me the difference between right and wrong. *Fortunately, the things they taught me were based on the Word of God* ... which was and still is my standard of conduct.

God expects us to do what is right in His sight. *He wants us to live our lives in such a way that we're doing what He wants ... not what we want or what others say is right.*

Isaiah 48:17 in the New Century Version says:

> *"This is what the Lord, who saves you, the Holy One of Israel, says: "I am the Lord your God, who teaches you to do what is good, who leads you in the way you should go."*

2.   When you do what is good you never repay evil with evil.

1 Thessalonians 5:15 in the New Century Version says:

> *"Be sure that no one pays back wrong for wrong, but always try to do what is good for each other and for all people."*

Not only that, but when you do what is good ... you will avoid evil.

Romans 16:19 in God's WORD Translation says:

> *"Everyone has heard about your obedience and this makes me happy for you. I want you to do what is good and to avoid what is evil."*

3.   Do what is good for other people.

1 Chronicles 19:13 in the Amplified Bible says:

"Be of good courage and let us behave ourselves courageously for our people and for the cities of our God; and may the Lord do what is good in His sight."

There is a scriptural reason why we should do good for others. It's found in 1 Corinthians 10:33 in the New Century Version and says:

"Just as I, also, try to please everybody in every way. I am not trying to do what is good for me but what is good for most people so they can be saved."

The primary reason that you do good for others is so they can be saved.

4. We should be ready to do what is good even if you don't agree with those involved.

This point will be hard for some people ... simply because they object to the policies of one administration and not another. I remember hearing those who criticized former President George W. Bush based on their interpretation of the scripture. Likewise, *I hear those who criticized former President Barack Obama based on their understanding of the Word, and President Trump is no different.*

I certainly have my opinions ... based on the Word of God; however, there is another part of the Word that says *we should submit to governmental authority and its leaders and that doesn't say only if we agree with them.* We should always be ready to do what is good in God's sight.

Titus 3:1 in the New Living Translation says:

> *"[Do What Is Good] Remind the believers to submit to the government and its officers. They should be obedient, always ready to do what is good."*

If you agree with a president, you want to pray for him. If you don't agree with a president, you need to pray for him! It is a win-win situation and it pleases God.

1 Timothy 2:1-3 in the Amplified Bible says:

> *"FIRST OF all, then, I admonish and urge that petitions, prayers, intercessions, and thanksgivings be offered on behalf of all men, For kings and all who are in positions of authority or high responsibility, that [outwardly] we may pass a quiet and undisturbed life [and inwardly] a peaceable one in all godliness and reverence and seriousness in every way. For such [praying] is good and right, and [it is] pleasing and acceptable to God our Savior."*

5. **When we obey God's Word ... things will be good with us.**

Deuteronomy 12:28 in the Amplified Bible says:

> "Be watchful and obey all these words which I command you, that it may go well with you and with your children after you forever, when you do what is good and right in the sight of the Lord your God."

Psalm 119:67-72 in the New Century Version says:

> "Before I suffered, I did wrong, but now I obey your word. You are good, and you do what is good."

Finally, Psalm 119:72 in the New Century Version reveals that His teachings are priceless.

> "Your teachings are worth more to me than thousands of pieces of gold and silver."

Seems to me the scripture is pretty clear … *if you follow His instructions things will go well with you even if you have a season of suffering thrown in before you get there.*

6. Sometimes when you do good your intentions may be misunderstood.

Psalm 38:20 in God's WORD Translation says:

> "They pay me back with evil instead of good, and they accuse me because I try to do what is good."

There are times when you offer to do something good but your intentions may be misunderstood or based on the level of revelation that you're walking in at the moment.

1 Chronicles 21:23 in the Amplified Bible says:

> "Ornan (oor non) said to David, Take it; and let my lord the king do what is good in his eyes. I give you the oxen also for burnt offerings and the threshing sledges for wood and the wheat for the meal offering. I give it all."

Ornan was concerned for his domain … or what was his when King David showed up with his men so he offered to provide what the King needed for his offering.

However, one of the most powerful passages of scripture is found in 1 Chronicles 21:24 in the Amplified Bible which says:

> "And King David said to Ornan, No, but I will pay the full price. I will not take what is yours for the Lord, nor offer burnt offerings which cost me nothing."

1 Chronicles 21:25 in the New International Version says:

> "So David paid Araunah six hundred shekels of gold for the site."

I double-clicked to view the commentary. That is when I discovered that 600 shekels of gold is the equivalent of 15 pounds of gold. There are sixteen ounces in a pound ... so David gave Araunah 240 ounces of gold.

Are you ready for this?

As of 2019, gold is selling for $1203.91 per ounce. So in today's prices, King David paid Araunah the equivalent of $288,712.80 for the land.

7. **When you do good ... you should never be moved by your personal circumstances, situations or problems.**

1 Peter 4:19 in God's WORD Translation says:

> *"Those who suffer because that is God's will for them must entrust themselves to a faithful creator and continue to do what is good."*

The nature of your adversity, regardless of how severe, should never hinder you from doing good for those who believe.

Galatians 6:10 in God's WORD Translation says:

> *"Whenever we have the opportunity, we have to do what is good for everyone, especially for the family of believers."*

When people talk about Harold Herring ... I want them to be reminded of Galatians 6:10. How about you?

7 Reasons Fear Destroys the Anointing

Fear is the devil's anointing.

Now I want you to write in the following statement where you can see it … remember it … believe it … confess it … until it's manifested in your life.

Fear is the devil's anointing but I rebuke it. Fear has no place in <<Name>>'s life.

Paul, Angela, Derreck, Shelia …

Make no mistake about it … the enemy will continually try to bring fear into your mental thought process.

Have you ever known anyone who was a prisoner of war?

I've had the honor of getting to know some brave men who were taken captive by the enemy and *endured the horrors of being a prisoner of war.* These men will tell you that the enemy creates an environment for brainwashing.

The enemy tries to break down their resistance ... by feeding them a consistent diet of hopelessness and fear. The enemy controls the interrogation process with just one objective ... break the captive's will to live ... so they will abandon their sense of right and wrong.

The devil would like nothing better than to make you a mental prisoner of war. He tries to create an atmosphere of panic and uncertainty ... *then he will bring negative thoughts into your mind ... trying to make you think you have no way of escape. He wants to replace your faith with fear ... your determination with his doubt ... your past with his future for you.*

The enemy of your success ... of *your anointing* ... wants fear in your life ... and he understands that you were born with two fears: *falling and loud noises*. All other fears are acquired.

Often deeply embedded within us, *fear results from past failures, from a lack of confidence bred unknowingly by our parents or relatives,* and *it's enforced by society's general negative, short-sighted thinking.*

Your loving Heavenly Father understands the strategies of the enemy. *He knows that if the enemy has you living in fear ...* that he can destroy the anointing on your life.

God wants us to understand that fear is not of Him.

Question ... how many times does God have to tell us something for us to believe it?

Once should be enough.

Would it be fair to say that if God wants you to really get something ... He will say it more than once?

In the King James Version of the Bible we're told nine times that we should be "born again."

So I think it's fair to say that being born again is significant and obviously important to God. After all, *He paid the ultimate price by sending His only begotten Son that we should not perish but have everlasting and abundant life ... by being born again.*

Would it surprise you to know that in the King James Version of the Bible ... we are told SIXTY-THREE times to "fear not"?

Let's look at some of those verses.

First, God wants us to eliminate all fear of failure.

Joshua 8:1 says:

> "And the LORD said unto Joshua, <u>Fear not</u>, neither be thou dismayed: take all the people of war with thee, and arise, go up ..."

Second, God wants us to know that He is our salvation so we have not reason to be fearful or

afraid.

Psalm 27:1 says:

> *"THE LORD is my Light and my Salvation-- whom shall I fear or dread? The Lord is the Refuge and Stronghold of my life--of whom shall I be afraid?"*

Third, God doesn't want to us worried or fearful about what might happen tomorrow.

Romans 8:32 in the New Living Translation says:

> *"Neither death nor life, neither angels nor demons, neither our fears for today nor our worries about tomorrow—not even the powers of hell can separate us from God's love."*

Are you seeing this? Neither the "fears for today nor our worries about tomorrow" can keep His love from you, *His promises from you* or His anointing for you from manifesting in your life. He is faithful to perform all that He has promised you if you receive it.

I think it's also important to get what Matthew 6:34 in the Message Bible says:

> *"Give your entire attention to what God is doing right now, and don't get worked up about what may or may not happen tomorrow. God will help you deal with whatever hard things come up when the time comes."*

Fourth, God is your helper so there's no need to fear.

Hebrews 13:5-6 in the Amplified Bible says:

> "So we take comfort and are encouraged and confidently and boldly say, The Lord is my Helper; I will not be seized with alarm [I will not fear or dread or be terrified]. What can man do to me?"

Fifth, fear will flee when God takes you by the hand.

Isaiah 41:9-10 in the Message Bible says:

> "Don't panic. I'm with you. There's no need to fear for I'm your God. I'll give you strength. I'll help you. I'll hold you steady, keep a firm grip on you."

Sixth, God is fighting against your enemies with you … so you have no reason to fear.

Deuteronomy 20:1 in the Message Bible says:

> "… In a few minutes you're going to do battle with your enemies. Don't waver in resolve. Don't fear. Don't hesitate. Don't panic. God, your God, is right there with you, fighting with you against your enemies, fighting to win."

Exodus 23:22 says:

> "But if you will indeed listen to and obey His voice … I will be an enemy to your enemies and an adversary to your adversaries."

Romans 8:31 in the Amplified Bible says:

> "… if God is for us, who [can be] against us? [Who can be our foe, if God is on our side?]"

Psalm 118:6 in the Message Bible says:

> "God's now at my side and I'm not afraid; who would dare lay a hand on me?"

Hebrews 13:6 in the Amplified Bible says:

> "So we take comfort and are encouraged and confidently and boldly say, The Lord is my Helper; I will not be seized with alarm [I will not fear or dread or be terrified]. What can man do to me?"

Seventh, you have no reason to be afraid because of the anointing that's living within you.

You have the Holy Spirit … teaching you how to manifest the anointing in your daily life.

John 14:26-27 in the Amplified Bible says:

> "But the Comforter (Counselor, Helper, Interces-

sor, Advocate, Strengthener,), the Holy Spirit, Whom the Father will send in My name [in My place, to represent Me and act on My behalf], He will teach you all things. And He will cause you to recall (will remind you of, bring to your remembrance) everything I have told you. Peace I leave with you; My [own] peace I now give and bequeath to you. Not as the world gives do I give to you. Do not let your hearts be troubled, neither let them be afraid. [Stop allowing yourselves to be agitated and disturbed; and do not permit yourselves to be fearful and intimidated and cowardly and unsettled.]"

God not only teaches you … but He has embedded Christ's anointing deeply within you.

1 John 2:26 in the Message Bible says:

"I've written to warn you about those who are trying to deceive you. But they're no match for what is embedded deeply within you—Christ's anointing, no less! You don't need any of their so-called teaching. Christ's anointing teaches you the truth on everything you need to know about yourself and him, uncontaminated by a single lie. Live deeply in what you were taught."

I trust you fully comprehend what this scripture is saying to you.

You have the anointing of Christ deep inside you. The verse also says, *"Live deeply in what you were taught."*

One more thing ... you cannot co-exist with sin ... neither can fear and the anointing live in the same house. The way you think, speak and act will either reflect fear or your anointing, but not both.

7 Steps to a Righteous Life

Day 29

I never cease to be amazed at the things God reveals to us in His Word.

If you're not gaining *revelatory insight into the Word* … it's simply because *you're not spending enough time there.*

Without a doubt … *God wants you meeting Him in His place* … the Word.

As I was reading 1 Peter 1:13-15 … the Lord gave me seven steps for every believer to live a righteous life. The verse says:

> "Wherefore gird up the loins of your mind, be sober, and hope to the end for the grace that is to be brought unto you at the revelation of Jesus Christ; As obedient children, not fashioning yourselves according to the former lusts in your ignorance: But as he which hath called you is holy, so be ye holy in all manner of conversation."

1. Protect what you're reproducing in your

imagination.

The Greek word dianoia (dee ah noi a) (G1271) translated as *mind* in verse 13 is often translated as imagination in other scriptures.

According to Strong's Concordance, gird refers to

> **"… the practice of the Orientals, who in order to be unimpeded in their movements were accustomed, when starting a journey or engaging in any work, to bind their long flowing garments closely around their bodies and fastened them with a leather belt."**

In other words, they girded their clothes *to protect themselves while traveling* and to allow unencumbered movement.

Loins is an anatomical reference … referring to reproductive abilities.

So verse 13 could be amplified to say, **"Protect what you're reproducing in your imagination."**

Jeremiah 3:17 says:

> *"… neither shall they walk any more after the imagination of their evil heart."*

An unrestrained thought is where compromise and sin begin … both are hindrances to a righteous life.

2. Being sober isn't the opposite of being drunk.

If someone were to ask if you were sober ... you might be insulted ... especially *if you didn't consume alcoholic beverages.*

In contemporary America, the word sober has come to denote someone who is not intoxicated. *If you say someone is sober at the moment*, the implication would be *that they're frequently drunk.*

Let's establish that scripturally speaking being sober isn't the opposite of being drunk.

According to Strong's Concordance the word sober means:

> **"to be sober, to be calm and collected in spirit; to be temperate, dispassionate, circumspect."**

The Greek word for sober appears seven times in six verses according to the Hebrew Concordance of the King James Bible.

One of those times is found in 1 Peter 5:8 which says:

> *"Be sober, be vigilant; because your adversary the devil, as a roaring lion, walketh about, seeking whom he may devour."*

Interestingly enough, the Message Bible translation of

1 Peter 5:8 refers to sober as "keeping a cool head."

3. Grace is so much more than what you say at a meal.

1 Peter 1:13 in the Amplified Bible says:

"... set your hope wholly and unchangeably on the grace (divine favor) that is coming to you when Jesus Christ (the Messiah) is revealed."

Now we all know that grace means "divine favor" when it refers to salvation. However, it means much more than this in many other places in your Bible.

The original Greek word for grace is CHARIS. (har ris)

The Greek Bible Dictionary defines it as:

"the divine influence upon the heart (and) its reflection in (a) person's life. Including acceptability, benefits, favor, gifting, and pleasure" or more simply said "grace, favor, anointings and divine enablings".

Notice with me that the Apostle Peter tells us that there are many forms of grace.

1 Peter 4:10 in the Amplified Bible says:

"Each of you have received a gift (a particular spiritual talent, a gracious divine endowment) as

... good trustees of God's many sided grace - faithful stewards of the extremely diverse power and gifts granted to Christians by unmerited favor (grace)."

Ephesians 3:7-8 in the Amplified Bible says:

"Of this [Gospel] I was made a minister according to the gift of God's free grace (undeserved favor) which was bestowed on me by the exercise (the working in all its effectiveness) of His power. 8 To me, though I am the very least of all the saints (God's consecrated people), this grace (favor, privilege) was granted and graciously entrusted: to proclaim to the Gentiles the unending (boundless, fathomless, incalculable, and exhaustless) riches of Christ [wealth which no human being could have searched out]."

These passages ought to excite you *about the possibilities in a righteous life* and *the favor and anointing that is available to you.*

4. Obedience brings rewards.

In the first part of 1 Peter 1:14 in the Amplified Bible, we are instructed to *"[Live] as children of obedience [to God] ..."*

I could do a number of teachings on the scriptural advisability of obedience but I'm just going to give you one scripture that makes our options pretty clear.

Isaiah 1:19 in The Living Bible says:

> "If you will only let me help you, if you will only obey, then I will make you rich."

If we let Him help us (our choice) ... *if we will obey (our choice)* ... then He will make you rich *(His choice and promise to us).*

5. Lust is a thought before it's ever an action.

The last part of 1 Peter 1:14 in the Amplified Bible says:

> "... do not conform yourselves to the evil desires [that governed you] in your former ignorance [when you did not know the requirements of the Gospel]."

As I was writing this the phrase from a song popped into my remembrance.

"Just one look ... that's all it took."

Matthew 5:28 says:

> "But I say unto you, That whosoever looketh on a woman to lust after her hath committed adultery with her already in his heart."

The Contemporary English Version of Matthew 5:28 says:

> "But I tell you that if you look at another woman

and want her, you are already unfaithful in your thoughts."

A righteous life becomes a reality by looking to a *more righteous future* and not living in the past.

6.   If you want to be like Him … you must think like Him.

The New Living Translation of 1 Peter 1:15 says:

"But now you must be holy in everything you do …"

How do you know what to do? … it's simple … do what the Word says.

A righteous life is a continual search for His presence and the revelation of His Word. When you want His Word more than anything else, then you're getting closer to the righteous life.

Paul wrote to young Timothy, *"… give attendance to reading …"* (1 Timothy 4:13) and, *"Study to show thyself approved … a workman that needeth not to be ashamed …"* (2 Timothy 2:15).

Hosea proclaimed, *"My people are destroyed (bound) for a lack of knowledge"* (Hosea 4:6). *It is interesting that Hosea did not say that Satan would destroy you. He stated that ignorance would destroy you.* Satan just helps you enjoy staying ignorant.

Ignorance of the Word is one of the greatest hindrances to a righteous life. *You must think like He thinks ... therefore you must know what He thinks.*

7.   Watch what you say.

One scripture is all this point needs. It's Ephesians 4:29 in the Amplified Bible which says:

> *"Let no foul or polluting language, nor evil word nor unwholesome or worthless talk [ever] come out of your mouth, but only such [speech] as is good and beneficial to the spiritual progress of others, as is fitting to the need and the occasion, that it may be a blessing and give grace (God's favor) to those who hear it."*

Now that you know the seven steps to a righteous life ... you don't have an excuse not to pursue it and live it if you want it.

RichThoughts for Breakfast

Volume 6

Invite Harold Herring to speak at your church, event, or rally.

Would you like to invite Harold to be a guest speaker at your church, event, or rally? Just send an email to:

booking@haroldherring.com

or call 1-800-583-2963

With a mix of humor, practical strategies, and Biblical insight Harold will inspire, encourage, and prepare you to change your financial destiny and set you on the path to not only set you free from debt but keep you free of debt and living the debt free life God has called you to.

Keep Thinking Rich Thoughts,

Harold Herring

RichThoughts for Breakfast

Jump Start Your Day!!

This motivating start to your day is something no one should be without. I guarantee you will be glad you called in.

Harold Herring

712-432-0900
Access Code 832936#
Playback Daily Call
712-432-0990
Access Code 832936#

The call starts at 8:30 AM EST seven days a week.

Practical Strategies, Biblical Insights and Thought-Provoking Humor

These are just a few of the things you are missing if you're not joining us every day for the **RichThoughts for Breakfast** morning call.

Get Ready to be Inspired, Encouraged, and Entertained.

Your Rich Thoughts are your leap to your future success!

Made in the USA
Lexington, KY
26 November 2019